Radical Self Love

A GUIDE TO LOVING YOURSELF
AND LIVING YOUR DREAM

GALA DARLING

4

Book and cover design: We Are Branch
wearebranch.com

Photographs: Made U Look Photography
madeulookphotography.com

Illustrations: Charlotte Thomson-Morley
charlottethomson.co.uk

ISBN: 978-0-692-44127-5

TABLE OF CONTENTS

ACKNOWLEDGMENTS

My life has been made so much better by the incredible women in it. This is for my babes.

Thank you: Shauna Haider who has been there since the beginning; Kat Williams for her tireless enthusiasm and encouragement; Emily Faulstich, who makes the world more beautiful; Veronica Varlow who is the most magic of all; Francesca Lia Block for always offering her support; Brandie Coonis for her thoughtful edits; Esmé Wang for making smart suggestions, and last but definitely not least, Janet Paape, who has always been my biggest cheerleader. I love you.

INTRODUCTION

---

t's a Full Moon, and I'm in New York City, soaking in a bath full of Epsom salts. There are candles burning, and the room smells like vanilla, lavender, and cocoa butter. I'm sitting sideways in the tub, my laptop perched precariously on the edge.

I'm so excited for you to dive into Radical Self Love: A Guide To Loving Yourself And Living Your Dream. This is a thrilling time for both of us! Picking up this book is the very first step towards creating a life of magic; a life that fills you with delight. Radical Self Love: A Guide To Loving Yourself And Living Your Dream is my take on how to fall in love with yourself and your life, two things I know a lot about.

Make no mistake: it took me a long time to get here. My body is covered in tattoos, scars from old piercings, scars from self-harm, all marking the passage of time. Don't think that I'm coming to you as someone who has always had it all figured out, because that is definitely not the case. Eight years ago, I was a completely different person. I was miserable, sick, and lost. I knew my life could be more than what it was, but I felt stuck. I had no idea how to get to where I wanted to be, and I let fear rule my life with an iron fist.

Maybe you identify with those sentiments. Perhaps you feel similarly bamboozled by the life you're living; maybe it doesn't look the way you expected. That's okay. Don't feel bad, or sad, or overwhelmed. We are going to start dismantling all those thoughts that no longer serve you, one by one!

No matter where you are in your journey of radical self love, I want you to know one thing: you always have the ability to change. In every moment, we're given an opportunity to evolve and grow, or shrink and stay stuck. You make the choice!

Take a second to tune into this precise moment. Maybe you, like me, are relaxing in the bathtub. Perhaps you're on the bus, listening to the squeak of windshield wipers and rain against the glass, or maybe you're sitting in your living room, cross-legged on your sofa, your dog slumbering quietly beside you.

I'm going to tell you something I know to be absolutely true. No matter where you are, and no matter what is going on around you, this is the only moment you ever have. Tomorrow may never come, and your past is long gone. The future, with all its promises and anxieties, may never eventuate. All you have is this moment, right here, and right now.

In this moment, you can create anything. It doesn't matter what you want to do, achieve, or experience: there are no limits. In this book, I am going to show you how to make your dreams a reality.

Now, fair warning: this ain't your mama's self-help book! We won't be listening to Enya, and you won't have to hide this book behind a copy of Vogue whenever you're in public. No, ma'am!

I've staked my claim on being wildly different, weird, and wonderful, so trust me when I say this book is going to get down and dirty fast. We're going to be diving into all things kooky and unconventional. We'll be talking about manifesting, masturbation, and making the mundane truly magical!

I believe that radical self love can go hand-in-hand with a ruby red lip. I believe that happiness can be cultivated. I believe that unless you fully love and appreciate yourself, your intimate relationships will be a shit-show of epic proportions. I believe that learning how to love yourself can be a party: streamers, disco balls, helium balloons and all!

I want you to realise your radiance. I want you to come to terms with your innate goddess nature. I want you to figure out how goddamn fabulous you are. The universe is waiting for you to step up and live out loud!

I'm absolutely thrilled to be presenting a real, live book: something you can hold in your hands, tuck into your handbag, and read until you fall asleep. Scribble notes in the margins, try the homework assignments, and document your adventures with #rslbook on Instagram and Twitter. I can't wait to see what you do next!

Thank you so much for joining me on this adventure. It has been an incredible ride so far. ♥

Ever,

LEARNING TO LOVE YOURSELF

Self-adoration, manifesting your
ideal persona, channelling your
inner Marie Antoinette and
everything in between!

Radical self love is my is my raison d'être, my passion, my mission. Exploring the concept, learning new tools, and putting them into practice fills me with so much excitement that I feel like my heart might explode! It's wonderful to experiment on yourself, to see what you can tweak to increase your happiness, but make no mistake, radical self love is vital stuff.

My mission is a personal one, and the reason I think radical self love is so valuable is because I have been to the other side -- something I like to call radical self loathing -- and back again. In my early twenties, my depression was so absolute that it rendered me almost entirely helpless. I was miserable, and to make matters worse, I was in the grips of an eating disorder too. My inner critic, the one who relentlessly told me how repulsive I was, had beaten me down so much that I had no fight left in me. Every day, I listened to that voice tell me what a terrible person I was, and I couldn't help but agree.

This was back in the days when Mary-Kate Olsen was in the tabloids every week, wearing 100 layers and carrying a Starbucks cup that was almost as big as she was. She was my "thinspiration", my idol. Nevermind the fact that she was 5'2", and I was 5'7", or the fact that we are built completely differently, or that aspiring to look like someone battling a serious illness is totally fucked up. My brain told me I should look like her, so why didn't I?

I would nurse a soy latte all day long, then keep the empty Starbucks cups and pile them up in a pyramid on my table, like a freaky altar that testified to the fact that I wasn't eating. I was literally running on caffeine.

Even though I was full to the brim with wonderful dreams about what my life could be, it felt like I was looking at them through a dirty window. Outside, life seemed to glow in technicolour, but in my mind, I was plagued by hopelessness and a sense of desperation. I couldn't figure out how to move into something that would make me feel good.

Depression combined with an eating disorder is a fatal combination, and has the highest mortality rate of any mental illness. My mind was so twisted that even when I thought about eating with some sense of normalcy, the voice in my head told me that without my eating disorder, I would cease to be interesting. It would prove to the world how dull I really was. It told me that all great artists were depressed and suffering from mental illness. No one happy ever created anything beautiful, it said.

I was a complete mess, and I knew it. I was exhausted, and I wanted to just give up. Secretly, I hoped I would get sick enough that I'd go to hospital, and someone else would take care of me. I couldn't do it anymore.

I've come a long way since then, and this book will show you how I did it. But my personal experiences provided the gallons of gasoline I have poured into my cause. The knowledge that my life could have turned out completely differently is what motivates me to spread the word about radical self love.

Back then, in what I like to call "the bad old days", I always thought that happiness was a ridiculous notion. Surely, only an idiot could be satisfied in a world full of so much darkness and depravity! I have since discovered that the world is what you make it, and you are constantly having your inner world reflected back at you. I discovered that when you choose to focus on the positive, to count your blessings and actively look for the good in people and in the everyday, it is entirely transformative. It changes your life forever.

Make no mistake, your radical self love journey does not happen in a day. Learning to love yourself is one of the biggest challenges we will ever face, and the work is never finished. It is a continual, ongoing process.

Even those of us who feel like we're pretty far along on the journey need a reminder every now and then. I feel like I need a daily prompt to be better to myself, more gentle, more forgiving, more accepting of myself and others. But the beauty of this work is that even though we are all starting from different places, we still need to learn and implement similar lessons.

A great place to start is by taking a good, clear look at what it means to love yourself. Sometimes we get confused, and think self-love is egotistical, vain, or self-obsessed. I can tell you right now: it ain't!

Radical self love is treating yourself the way you would treat your very best, most treasured friend. Our friends aren't perfect, and we know it (oh boy, do we know it), but we love them anyway. Your best friend might get into a ridiculous flap over some boy you think is nowhere near good enough for her, or talk about wanting to go to Paris but never save any money, and you still love her. You think she is a cosmic gift: a shooting star in the shape of a girl. This is how we should choose to view ourselves, too.

In metaphysics, we learn that like attracts like, which means that your life will be filled with the things that you believe you deserve. Think about your friends, for example. What do their lives look like? Are they happy, fulfilled, successful? If they're not, you probably aren't either. We are the average of the five people we spend the most time with!

Radical self love -- or the lack of it -- works in a loop. If you don't think much of yourself, it emanates from you in waves. The stench of self-loathing is all over you, and you'll find yourself unconsciously attracting people into your life who are unhappy, self-sabotaging, or manipulative. Sometimes those people can sniff it out, knowing subconsciously that they can treat you badly and you'll come back for more. This only gives you more fodder for personal disapproval, negative self-talk and unhappiness.

On the flipside, people who embrace radical self love set goals and go for them. They attract people into their lives who are intelligent, fun, inspiring, and positive. Their life is fulfilling, and they're able to enjoy themselves anywhere. They don't judge other people for the personal choices they've made, instead accepting and embracing the fact that everyone is different. They make decisions on their own terms and they don't allow their family, friends, society, or well-meaning strangers to dictate how they should live.

One of the most destructive beliefs I've observed is that cynicism, sarcasm and a judgmental attitude are a way of proving your intellect. I can say this with some authority, since it's what I used to believe! As I said earlier, like attracts like, so if you go around remarking on everything that pisses you off, don't be surprised when you wake up in the morning and feel miserable. Don't be shocked by the fact that everything in your life feels crappy, and that you can never find a lover who treats you right. All of this stuff comes from not loving yourself. Truly.

Everything we do in life comes from a place of fear, or a place of love. How often do you think you allow fear to motivate you? How many times a day do you act from a place of love?

One thing I was shocked to learn when I started shedding my nasty old beliefs was that it's much easier to be negative than positive. Any old fool can find something to moan about, but it takes skill and effort to see the good in life. Being happy requires strength and intelligence. Anyone can be judgmental, sour, resentful, and cantankerous, but it takes real mental discipline, tenacity, and vigor to change your mindset, and to see the positive in a world which can be so messed up.

Make no mistake, the concept of changing your world-view is a biggie! You wouldn't be alone if you were daunted and intimidated by the thought. I mean, where the hell do you even begin?

You start small, and you start with one thing, because you can't change the world until you've choked out your own demons. How do you do that? Let me tell you...

TOP SECRET WEAPONS IN THE FIGHT AGAINST SELF-LOATHING

#radicalselflovedate

Begin by learning to get comfortable spending time alone. I recommend everyone goes on a #radicalselflovedate -- an adventure for one -- at least once a week. Maybe you could go to lunch by yourself, or see a movie alone. You could go for a drive, or a walk through the park... It could be anything! The only condition is that you do it solo.

A lot of us feel anxious about doing this kind of thing: we worry that other people will stare at us or think we're freaky, but trust me, no one else cares what you are doing. They are so concerned with their uncomfortable underpants or financial messiness that they have no mental capacity available to judge you! And even if they were judging you, so what?! Why does their opinion matter? Remember, what other people think about you is none of your business!

One of the most pressing reasons to take yourself on a #radicalselflovedate is to help you get back to yourself; to assist you in rediscovering who you really are. We all have such short attention spans these days, and we are constantly distracted. Music, television, advertising, phone-calls, text messages, Twitter, email, books, newspapers, movies: the list goes on and on, and while all of these things have their purpose and can be fabulous, what they have in common is that they pull us away from ourselves, our true centre. The time we spend emailing or watching television is time that we are not committing to simply being. Indulging in these distractions is a way of escaping ourselves, so we don't have to think about who we are, or be present, or really settle into ourselves. So many of us can barely stand spending time by ourselves in a room with no distractions. We feel compelled to change songs, tidy up, check our email, or send a text message, but this doesn't help us. It just delays us doing the work on ourselves, and learning to get really comfortable with who we are.

Isn't it time to fall in love with yourself? I say yes!

That's my first prescription for you (just call me Doctor [Radical Self] Love)! Take yourself on a #radicalselflovedate this week, then report back by using the hashtag on Twitter or Instagram!

Meditation

Okay, don't freak out. You don't have to sit with your legs criss-crossed next to a gong in an all-white room to experience the benefits of meditation: it can be as simple as taking five minutes to sit in silence. You don't have to become a Zen master, I promise!

Meditation is about training what is called the "monkey mind". Monkey mind is what I outlined above: that constant urge to think, churn, do things, and distract ourselves from just existing. Meditation is actually very simple in concept -- you sit down, take some deep breaths, and do nothing -- but it's much more challenging than it sounds, which you'll know if you've ever tried it yourself!

A few years ago, I would have advised you to just plop your butt on a cushion, close your eyes, and give it a shot, but these days we have the wonder of technology to help us! Instead of sitting in silence, try doing a guided meditation, where someone leads the way by giving you physical sensations to observe, or talks you through a relaxing visualisation.

If you want to make it really simple, you can even download an app to your phone to help! One of my favourites is called Headspace, and it leads you through a series of ten minute meditations. YouTube is also a fantastic source for any kind of meditation you can imagine. Do a little browsing and see what you find!

Another trick I have? I smile while I meditate. It feels silly at first, but it quickly begins to generate a whole slew of really positive feelings. Our physiology informs our psychology, so smiling even when you don't feel like it will actually make you happy! Incredible, no?

Sometimes people will say to me, "I tried meditating, but I just can't. There's too much stuff in my mind!" Okay, well, that's the whole point! Everyone has too much stuff in their head, that's why meditation is so powerful. Very few people can have a completely clear head while they sit. As you meditate, your mind will constantly throw things at you -- items on your to-do list, ponderances about that cute boy or girl, things you should really write down, questions about how much longer you're meant to sit there -- but just let them pass. Don't judge your thoughts, reprimand yourself for thinking them, or indulge them. Just observe them and let them float past.

The good news is that you don't have to meditate for very long to reap the benefits. Research has shown that meditating for 12 minutes a day improves memory scores, in addition to decreasing anger and anxiety. Even five minutes when you wake up or just before you go to sleep is a really wonderful way to start!

People who have been meditating for a long time have much higher activity in the frontal lobes of their brain, which is the part that helps focus our attention and will. (Translation: laser focus and extreme willpower can be yours for the taking!) It's all very cool. If you just do a little bit of research, you'll learn about the multitude of ways in which meditation can change your life!

Tapping

When people ask me where I got started with radical self love, the answer is simple: tapping. I started using this technique back in 2006, when it was not well known, and very fringe. These days, it's a commonly-utilised technique, and is used and enthusiastically raved about by thought-leaders like Kris Carr and Gabrielle Bernstein.

Tapping is an energetic healing technique, similar to acupuncture or acupressure in that it makes use of pressure points and meridians in the body to help clear emotional blockages. I love tapping, because it's extremely easy, and best of all, it costs nothing! All you do is repeatedly press on various parts of your body while talking out loud about the problem or issue you're trying to resolve.

Now, I know this sounds bizarre. Believe me, I do, because when I first heard about it, I thought it was the tallest tale on the planet. I was introduced to it by a boyfriend who would spend hours sitting in a corner, tapping and muttering to himself. I thought it was beyond weird, and no matter how much he told me about the great results he was getting from it, I was extremely skeptical. I was convinced that something so simple could never work, and that it had to be placebo effect.

Eventually, after listening to him bang on and on about it, I decided to give it a try. Because I was extremely cynical, I decided I wanted proof. I wanted to tap on something that would give me an accurate reading, proving that either it had worked, or it had not. I wanted to tap on something I couldn't fool myself about, so I chose asthma as my first target.

Ever since I was a little girl, I had terrible asthma. It was triggered by almost everything: cats, changes in temperature, exercise, dust... You name it, and I was reaching for my inhaler. At the time, I was working at New Zealand Post and living in the centre of Auckland city, and every morning, I had to walk up a hill to take the bus. Without fail, I'd be grasping for my inhaler.

That night, I sat down, and as my boyfriend coached me, I tapped on having an asthma attack and needing to use my inhaler.

Imagine my surprise when, the morning after tapping, my asthma was gone. I walked up the hill to catch the bus with absolutely no need to use my inhaler. I was completely astounded. This was not placebo effect, it was real. It opened my mind up in a way that shocked me, and I became an instant convert. For the next few months, I tapped on everything in my life that I didn't want anymore, including depression, hayfever, cat allergies, chronic back pain, and most dramatically, the eating disorder that had haunted me for years.

It took me quite some time to muster up the courage to face my eating disorder head-on. My illness was my identity; I was terrified to let it go. My eating disorder played tricks on me, lying to me and telling me anything to keep me trapped. It knew my trigger points. Mine told me that if I was happy, I wouldn't be able to be creative; that a sad, thin girl was so much more "interesting" than a happy, healthy girl. It told me that happiness was boring, that seeing food as nourishment rather than the enemy would make me mediocre, un-special. But I felt desperate and out of control; I had to do something. I decided to take charge, even though I was petrified, even though I wondered if, without my illness, I would have any personality left.

I didn't have a strategy or a plan, and I had no idea whether tapping on something so huge would have any effect. I just did what felt right to me. I walked into the bathroom, locked the door, took off my clothes, and stood in front of the mirror. I looked into my eyes and talked about how I felt about myself and my body while I tapped. In some ways, I couldn't believe what was coming out of my mouth. It's one thing to hear it in your head for years, but it's entirely another to say it out loud. I started crying almost immediately, and at one point I was so hysterical that I couldn't even get any words out. Still, I kept going. I kept tapping.

Tapping is a strange thing because at some point in the process, you feel an internal shift, and you realise the issue has either changed, or -- in some cases -- disappeared completely. I felt a shift. Something was different. I stopped crying all of a sudden, and I felt calm. In that mirror, I saw something unfamiliar and new.

My body was filled with a feeling of euphoria. You know how, after a really good cry, you feel extra-calm? It was like that, times a hundred. I put my clothes back on, and walked into the living room where my boyfriend was sitting. I told him what had happened, and I was in the middle of explaining what had happened, when I was hit with a wave of nausea. I ran to the bathroom and threw up, violently, over and over again. I am convinced that this was my body affirming what I had just done. In no uncertain terms, my body was saying, "I want all of these feelings gone!"

The next day, I was able to eat without guilt, and in fact, I have never felt any shame or terror about food since then. I can describe it as nothing less than a miracle. Now that my issues around food had vanished into thin air, I started to tackle my body image. This was much less difficult, and I simply tapped on those individual aspects when they came up. Even though I still had work to do, that night I spent in front of the mirror completely changed my life. I have never since felt the need to gulp diet pills or subsist on a cup of coffee a day, and I can't put into words how thankful I am.

I'm also delighted to report that my eating disorder was wrong. Being happy is awesome, and I am so much more creative, adventurous, interesting, prosperous and fulfilled than I could have ever imagined. I also uncovered my true personality. I always thought I would be cynical until the end, and mercifully, that was not the case. I am a true optimist, full of hope and the ability to look on the bright side of pretty much everything. Discovering all of this has been nothing short of magical.

The best thing about tapping is that once you've used it to clear out any really major issues, you can use it to keep tweaking and improving your quality of life, to make you happier, more positive and more productive. It is the very best tool in my arsenal, and since writing about it on my website, one of my favourite things is to receive emails from people who have tried it with fantastic results.

A woman wrote to me saying she had never had an orgasm, ever, and had even booked an appointment with a doctor just to make sure there was nothing wrong with her physically. The night before the appointment, she recalled my article about tapping, and decided to give it a go. She tapped on the fact that she had never been able to have an orgasm, and a couple of days later, she had her first orgasm ever. And her second. And her third. And her fourth, fifth, sixth and seventh! That night, her boyfriend came over, and she had twelve orgasms in a row! Hallelujah! Talk about making up for lost time!

While the whole concept of tapping sounds kind of silly and unlikely to most of us, even to me in the beginning, I always feel like it's something worth trying. If you don't find that it works -- and I haven't met a single person yet for whom it hasn't worked -- all you've lost is a little bit of time. It's not like it costs money or requires you to do anything super-embarrassing in public, it's just you in your bedroom doing a bit of experimentation. It's worth giving it a shot simply because it could change your life.

Because tapping is physical, I think it's easiest to just show you how to do it. To learn how to tap, watch my free video -- galadarling.com/article/eft -- or check out galadarling.com/tapthat

Body love

Research has shown that women spend an average of 55 minutes a day in front of the mirror. Sometimes we're just brushing our teeth or fixing our hair, but how much of that time is spent getting up close and personal with our pores, fretting over a pimple, or wishing we looked like someone else?

When was the last time you looked in a full-length mirror and liked everything you saw?

My babe, it is time to wake up, because we've been sold a lie. It breaks my heart to hear the statistics about how young girls would rather be "thin" or "famous" than be an astronaut. Size 0 is a marketing tactic! Big businesses profit from our physical distress, selling us diet pills, stockings that compress your jiggly bits, endless cosmetics, gym memberships, and fake foods made in a laboratory so you can "eat yourself skinny". I could go on about this forever, but I won't. Just know that businesses profit -- and CEOs take home multi-million dollar salaries -- when we buy into the lie they sell us.

The struggle to be thin is an internal battle played out on the exterior. You may think that you want to look different, but what you really want is to feel different. Being skinny doesn't change your life, and it doesn't make you happy or fulfilled. Being healthy is one thing -- yes, being strong and fit will transform how you feel about yourself -- but being a teeny-tiny stick figure is not the path to enlightenment.

In fact, the opposite is true. If you're starving yourself, you're the antithesis of a contented person. You will be -- and I feel justified in saying this, because I've been there -- insufferably boring, not to mention miserable. People who don't eat are so grumpy! Your body needs food to stay alive. It is not something you can choose to skip without suffering serious consequences. Your biggest problem right now might be a bad mood, but the repercussions are grim to say the least. If you stay on that path, your hair and teeth will fall out, you'll be unable to walk, and your organs will start failing. In my humble opinion, it's just not worth it.

Beyond using tapping to help you deal with body image issues as they come up, the thing that has helped me learn to LOVE my body is exercise. When I was sick, I used to go on long, punishing runs, thinking about how fat I was the whole time. There was no enjoyment in it, it was a gloomy display. These days, I go to the gym five days a week -- two days of Pilates, three days of weight training -- and I absolutely adore it. It's the quickest way to transform my mood, and I can see myself growing stronger and more capable every day.

The gym isn't for everyone, though. Experiment with different activities, and see what helps you get your kicks! You might love going to yoga classes and having a great stretch, hula-hooping to your favourite tunes, or flying through the air at trapeze classes.

Sometimes just knowing we're making the effort to use our body can make us feel 200% better about ourselves. Plus, exercise releases endorphins and adrenaline which is an instant, totally natural high.

If the idea of exercise makes you want to puke, don't sweat it! A great way to get in touch with your body, literally, is to masturbate more! It's the very definition of self-love, and who could fail to be amazed by the marvellous act of orgasm?!

Think about your body language and posture, too. Straighten your back, drop your shoulders and hold your head high. Smiling, even when we're grumpy, sends a message to the brain that we're happy! Standing up straight has the same effect on our psyche. Lengthen your neck, raise your chin, channel Nefertiti and watch your life evolve!

Taking action

My father always told me that one of the best ways to build self-esteem is to take on challenges, see them through, and achieve things you're proud of. He is fond of the phrase "get some successes under your belt." Of course, he is right!

When it comes to learning how to love yourself, start small. If your first challenge is to climb Everest, you'll feel overwhelmed, and that will add to your discontent. Instead, do something simple. Maybe you could commit to a week of meditation, or buy a pair of sneakers and go for a run once a week, or pay your bills as soon as they come in. These little successes will build up, and help add to your positive view of yourself.

Once you've achieved something, set yourself a new goal and go for it! Goal-setting is essential for encouraging your self-esteem to flourish. It will make you realise that you have value, purpose, and unique talents to offer!

✷ ✷ ✷

MANIFESTING YOUR IDEAL PERSONA

When I was born, my parents named me Amy. Years later, when I asked them why, they said, "We didn't want you to have a nickname." (They named my siblings Sarah and Paul, so let's just say, creative naming was not their strong suit.)

I always disliked the name Amy. It never spoke to me, it never really said anything about who I was. I'd pore over books of baby names and their meanings, wishing I was an Aurora ("goddess of the sunrise"), Momoe ("hundred blessings") or Cynthia ("the moon personified"). Amy meant "beloved". Yawn! My name was so common, in fact, that I was only one of several Amys in my class at school. I was "Amy P", as opposed to "Amy S" or "Amy T". Awful.

When I first started exploring the internet in 1996, it was my chance to be whomever I wanted... And I went for it. I dived head-first into the world of nicknames and handles, trying out anything which came into my head. My first nickname was TheWizard, before moving onto BloodRose (hello, goth phase); Ponderosa, and my pièce de résistance, Fuckerina. Charming, right?

Around about 2003, I started calling myself Gala online. I don't remember where it came from, though I'm sure Salvador Dalí's wife was a persuasive influence. The more I called myself Gala, the more I liked it, and I began to realise how little I identified with the name on my birth certificate.

I decided I wanted to change my name. I didn't know what I wanted it to be, or even if Gala would be part of it, but I set the intention that I wanted a name to come to me. That same month, I awoke from a daytime catnap and wrote down, "I just woke up from a dream where my name was GALA LUMIÈRE DARLING."

The physical act of changing my name was easy: I printed some forms, filled them out, and sent them off with a cheque for $150. But the emotional act of changing my name was transformative.

I had gone from having a name no one ever noticed to a name that everyone had an opinion on. "Gala? That's so pretty!" "Gala, like, a party?" "I wish my last name was Darling!"

And it wasn't just that. Gala Lumière Darling was a very big name. It had promise, it had potential, it sparkled and sizzled and pulsed with light. It was magical, and I loved it, but it was too big for me at the time. It was so bombastic and supersonic that I was almost intimidated by it.

I realised that I would feel totally ridiculous registering for unemployment with a name like that -- which I had done at least twice before, while between multiple sucky jobs -- and that it was time to cough up and deliver something. Maybe it was time to start living my dreams after all. Tremble!

When you have a name that people exclaim over when they look at receipts or while making an appointment, you feel the pressure to live up to that, and expand on who you are. Ultimately, it was good for me. I needed a little nudge to step it up, and my name was a major piece of that puzzle.

My belief is that names are like lovers or clothing -- sometimes we outgrow them, and there's nothing wrong with leaving them in the past as you stride boldly into the future. Who knows, I might change my name again one day, to something that suits me better at the time. Why not, right?

Of course, changing your name is on the more extreme end of the spectrum when it comes to developing your own distinctive persona, but you can take this concept and expand it in any direction you like. Changing your name is one option, sure, but you could give yourself a new nickname, switch up your saunter, dress differently, speak more slowly... You get the idea. You can truly be anyone you want!

Feeling intimidated? Just start small. Channel your mother when you get dressed, or think like your aunt when you're doing business. Then let it swell, and make it bigger. Think Madonna's ego, Donald Trump's ambition, Marie Antoinette's commitment to decadence! Sometimes your attempts at channelling someone you admire will fall flat, but that's okay. One of my ex-boyfriends was fond of saying that failure happens to everyone, but the best thing we can do is to fail a lot and fail QUICKLY, and just keep moving, learning and developing.

One of the easiest ways to assess how much you love yourself is to simply look at the choices you're making in your everyday life. Ultimately, everything we do is an offshoot of our own self-esteem, and is a working testament to how much we value ourselves. If you don't value yourself very highly, your lifestyle will reflect that. Maybe you're constantly hanging out with negative people, or you're a compulsive procrastinator, or you live on a diet of saturated fats and bourbon.

Our brain's primary function is to make sense of and justify everything in our lives, good or bad. Humans are amazing at this; we can excuse and rationalise everything. Yes, you can justify and defend your bad behaviour until the cows come home, but deep down, you know that this is not what you would be doing if you really, really loved yourself.

Before you beat yourself up about it, fear not: no one has this stuff perfectly worked out. Radical self love is a work in progress, and no matter how golden your intentions, we all make choices from time to time which let us down. You might put off exercising, watch five hours of reality television instead of reading a book, stay in relationships which have long since passed their expiry date, and the list goes on and on. That's okay.

A massive and essential part of self-love is forgiveness and acceptance. So while you're making an effort and striving to be the best person you can be, at the same time you need to recognise your own humanity. Try not to hold yourself to impeccable standards, and just do the best you can right now.

Clearly, most of this is internal work, which at first sounds like it could be an epic drag, but when you get your head around it, you'll realise that it is totally empowering. It gives you the opportunity to become whomever you want; to channel the parts of other people, characters, even myths, and bring them together into the person you are. There is nothing wrong with doing this, and everyone does it to some degree or another.

After all, life is not about finding yourself, it is about creating yourself, and when we go through this process there is a certain amount of borrowing, trying on, adopting and discarding which occurs. If you ask any great artist who has influenced them, they will be quick to rattle off a list of names, and you can bet that many of the things they do today are an offshoot of things they learned from others. Now, this is not to say that you should be a facsimile of someone else, definitely not -- that isn't being true to yourself, that's hiding yourself behind something inauthentic. But there is massive value in looking around, observing what you like in others, writing down lists of ideal character traits, and trying out new sets of behaviours.

If you think about the great people in this world -- the Oscar Wildes, the Diana Vreelands, the Twiggys and Albert Einsteins -- you will realise that what makes them so wonderful is their uniqueness! The really incredible people who make an impact and go on to inspire others are like a hyperreal version of a normal person. Their characters are so overdeveloped that it almost seems like a caricature.

We all have the ability to expand our persona in that sort of direction, but it doesn't happen overnight. Your uniqueness will require time to percolate. We are all born beautiful, unusual and wild, but it takes time to refine, to marinate, and for those facets to take on a new shape. Even if you're not aware of it, we are all constantly evolving: adopting new interests, affectations, phrases, ways of moving... If you're not growing and changing and trying new things, what's the point?

Think back on yourself 5 years, 2 years, even 6 months ago. I'm sure you are not the same person. Wonderful, tragic and unusual things will have happened in that time which have shaped you into the person you are today, sitting here, reading this. Change is inevitable, and even though the way it happens isn't always pretty, it propels us forward onto something better and more fantastic. Metamorphosis makes our life brighter, bigger, bolder and more lovely, so don't be afraid of change. Don't be nervous about loving yourself, or admitting that you want something better.

In terms of the type of person you are, or can be, I sincerely believe the sky's the limit (as Notorious B.I.G. would say). After all, incredible people have to come from somewhere: why not your house?

The first step is to switch up the way we think about ourselves. It's pretty common to believe that we're just going to end up like our parents, but once you get hip to the fact that you can create your own life, those thoughts become as dated as disco! You can live the life of your dreams, and it's disempowering to think any other way.

Think about the infinite power and possibilities of the universe. Who says we can't harness that kind of juice to create the life we want? My life is total testament to that, and yours can be too! For every "No, that's impossible" I hear from someone with a downturned mouth, I can think of a thousand real-life situations to disprove it... and I leave the doubters in my fuchsia pink wake!

So who do you want to be, and what do you want to have in your life? Do you want to be well- dressed, outspoken, brave, and spontaneous? Do you want to play tennis, learn how to rock a drumkit, and go swimming every morning? It's never too late to start! All you need to do is make a choice and then start LIVING in that direction! It may take time for all the pieces to fall in place, but even that isn't necessarily true. You can date anyone, do whatever you want for work, live in any city which takes your fancy, and dress however you like. All it takes is a decision and some conscious action.

Any old fool can find something to moan about, but it takes skill and effort to see the good in life. Being happy requires strength and intelligence.

#RSLBOOK

HOMEWORK

♥ LET'S EMBRACE #RADICALSELFIELOVE!

Selfies can be a wonderful form of self-expression. When you take a self-portrait, you're showing the world how you want to be seen, which is powerful. Take photos of yourself, and get comfortable with how you look. Take photos of your least favourite body parts, and don't share them with anyone. Just look at the pictures regularly, and see if you can learn to love them.

♥ TRY TAPPING.

It's the fastest way to clear negative thoughts and habits out of your life. Why hold onto harmful feelings and actions? Tap on it and let it go, so you can move forward and become the person you've always wanted to be. I have a free demonstration video at galadarling. com/article/eft, or you can learn along with me at home! Just go to galadarling.com/tapthat

♥ INCORPORATE NEW POSITIVE ATTRIBUTES INTO THE MIX.

Make a list of people who inspire you. Alongside their names, write down any attributes they possess that you admire. How could you infuse your life with those characteristics? Scribble down any ideas that come to mind, and then tape it up in your entrance-way. For example, if radiance is a characteristic you'd like to enjoy, maybe you could embody that by practicing good posture, wearing more colour, and smiling more often. If you'd like to be more assertive, work at saying "No" more readily, as well as asking for what you want.

♥ EXAMINE YOUR LIMITING BELIEFS.

Sometimes it can be difficult to figure out what your limiting beliefs are, because our limiting beliefs constitute our world view. Here's what I suggest: when you have a thought (and it could be about anything!), ask yourself, "Is that really true?" Here are some examples of limiting beliefs: all men are jerks; there are no fun creative jobs; no one's hiring; I'm doomed to be alone for the rest of my life; I'm always sick; things like this always happen to me. Make a note of any thought you'd like to change, and then tap on it!

❤ GET IN TOUCH WITH YOUR BODY.

In my Radical Self Love Salons, one thing I hear over and over again is that a lot of women feel disconnected from their bodies. Use it or lose (connection with) it! Sign up for a yoga class, bust out your running shoes, or just hula-hoop in your living room. Try meditating for 5 minutes. Walk on the grass. And if you've never had an orgasm, buy a vibrator, babe!

FINDING HAPPINESS AND MAKING IT STAY

Choosing joy, making magic
and devoting your life to love,
adventure and deliciousness!

Happiness is our natural state. Children are happy so much of the time, but as life continues, it's not unusual to get knocked off balance. Happiness becomes something elusive, something rare, or something we have to work for. We start to question it. Do we deserve to be happy? Can you be intelligent and still be happy? How can anyone feel happy when the world is in such a shambles? All of these questions as well as external circumstances leave us in a state of confusion, and don't bring us any closer to the feeling of happiness we all really, really want.

I believe that the most important thing you can do every day is feel good, because when you do, all good things will be attracted to you. The marvellous thing about happiness is that in a lot of ways, it's very easy. You can either choose a thought which makes you happy, or a thought that makes you anxious, and you can make that choice every moment of every day.

✳ ✳ ✳

WELCOME TO THE PRESENT MOMENT

Would you like to know a secret? This moment right now -- no matter where you are in the world -- is the only moment you ever have. Tomorrow may never come. Your past is gone. The future is a myth. There is nothing else. Just this.

Because this is all there is, it is the only thing you will ever have any control over. This might sound like I am reducing your life to a very small thing, but that is not the case. Everything is contained within the present moment. It is magical, blessed, and magnificently ALIVE. It is here. It has arrived.

Within this moment, you can do anything. You can create anything you want right now. You don't have to wait for permission from anyone else: you already have the power within you to change your life. You can harness the power of positive thought to draw beautiful things to you: love, prosperity, good health, and adventures of every stripe!

There is so much enchantment in the present moment, and the more aware of that we can be, the happier we will be.

Learning to truly be in the present moment is a marvellous skill to acquire, but it can take time. Eckhart Tolle has written extensively on this subject, and his books are a great place to go for more information, but you can start living in the moment right now! It's very easy: when your mind is going off the rails, and you are overwhelmed with thoughts, worries, or whatever it is that's in your head, take a moment to let it all go. Sometimes visualising letting go of it is easiest -- picture all your worries as a big brick or rock, and envision yourself throwing it over your shoulder, or off a building, or into the depths of the ocean. Then focus on your breath. Pay attention to it. See if you can make your inhale and exhale an equal length. Do that for as long as you can, and you will feel different. Your focus will have shifted; your awareness will have changed; you may find that you even have a totally different perspective. Do this as often as you can!

Practising meditation is another fantastic way to get really intimate with the present moment -- go back to Chapter One if you missed my write-up!

Learning to be in the present moment and discovering how to truly appreciate the present moment is one of the very best ways to seize the day. Carpe diem, ma cherie! When you make the effort to view every day as a fantastic, opportunity-laden treasure, you can really make the most of it, and the world will truly be yours.

LOOK AT YOUR PATTERNS

Happiness is not quite as simple as living in the present moment, however. We need to really look at ourselves and get a good view of what makes us tick, so that we can start changing the things that aren't working for us any more. A fantastic place to start is to examine your patterns.

Everyone has patterns. We start learning them in childhood, and most of us continue to operate within those parameters for the rest of our lives. They may be comfortable, but it takes only a little bit of insight to realise that we'd be better off without some of them.

What do I mean when I talk about patterns? Patterns are subconscious beliefs which dictate our behaviour. It's all about history repeating itself, and we see that happen all the time.

Here are some patterns you might recognise in your life.

♥ The I'm-constantly-running-late pattern. Some people could put the White Rabbit to shame: they are absolutely, categorically, always late, no matter the circumstances. This pattern can be so ingrained that even if they find themselves on time, they will subconsciously throw some kind of spanner in the works so that they are back behind schedule again!

♥ The drama pattern. This is strongly connected with not believing that you deserve to be happy. If things seem to be going well, these people will attract some kind of drama or crisis into their life, which further reinforces their belief that "life is hard".

♥ The sickness pattern. Some people believe that being under the weather is the status quo, and a lot of that is modelled after what you experienced in childhood. No matter where the belief began, you know that when you ask them how they are, they'll be quick to mention some kind of physical ailment!

♥ The I'm-always-broke pattern. These are people who will always find a way to spend any extra money they have. They spend themselves back to zero, or wherever it is that they're comfortable. This is why so many people who win the lottery go totally broke within a year or two: it doesn't feel right, so their subconscious mind works out a way to throw it all away.

♥ The people-are-always-horrible-to-me pattern. The people locked into this pattern can never get along with anyone, be it their family, their spouse's family, workmates or people they live with. You'll notice that it's never their fault, either!

♥ The I-am-always-in-the-wrong-place-at-the-wrong-time pattern. Let's just call this perpetual pessimism and be done with it!

♥ The just-my-luck pattern. Also known as the "I knew this would happen to me!" pattern. We get what we expect!

So how we do begin to change these patterns? Where do we start? After all, if we're always sick, or broke, or people are always awful to us, getting happy is going to be difficult. The good news is that none of these things are true, it's just that our minds make them true because we believe the story we tell ourselves!

Knowing is half the battle. Most of us are totally unaware that we operate on these programs, so of course we can't do anything about it! But if you know what's going on in that noodle of yours, you can start to change the old habits which support your patterns and keep them ticking along.

We're going to learn a bunch of ways of dismantling these old beliefs, so hold on tight!

TAKING RESPONSIBILITY

One of the major pieces of the puzzle when it comes to being happy is that you have to start taking responsibility for your life. 100% responsibility, in fact: radical responsibility! This is not up for debate! A lot of people can feel quite indignant when they first hear this, but it is really an essential part of being happy or fulfilled!

There are so many people who go through life blaming everyone but themselves, and they are never really very happy about anything. They feel like victims of life, just along for the ride as opposed to being the captain of their own ship. Life simply happens to them. They don't know what is coming next and they fear change. It makes sense that if you feel this way, you wouldn't experience much lasting joy. The brief snatches of delight would never last, because it would feel as if it was going to be snatched out from under you at any moment. Needless to say, this is no way to live!

Taking responsibility for yourself is quite terrifying, and even reading the words might make a lump form in your throat. Sometimes when people are confronted with the idea of taking responsibility for themselves, they become angry... Very angry. They will yell, scream, and list off ten million "perfectly logical" reasons why it wasn't their fault. But if you recognise that thoughts become things, and that we attract whatever it is we think about the most, you'll soon realise that everything that happens comes from us.

Our external world reflects our internal beliefs.

Gloria Steinem said, "The truth will set you free. But first, it will piss you off." Too true!

Some people, upon being told that they are responsible for 100% of their life, feel like they are being told, "This is all your fault, you are a bad person, and if you were not a bad person you would not have brought these things upon yourself." But that is not what they are being told at all. That is just their interpretation.

Here's the thing: none of us are taught this stuff. No one ever tells us that our thoughts create our life. We have no idea. We inherit our patterns of thinking from our parents, who inherit them from their parents, and so on. This generation of people is just now waking up to the fact that we manifest our own reality, and it is still new information, so don't feel that you are to blame because you never knew, or that you are at fault because you are just learning these things now. It's okay. Think of this as a crash course, a dazzling introduction to a new galaxy of possibility!

Now you know, so how can you put it into action? How can you start owning up to the choices you've made in your life? There are lots of little ways to begin, and they all involve a simple change in thinking. For example, instead of blaming your ex-boyfriend for ruining your life, take responsibility for allowing him into your life in the first place, and for wreaking his own unique brand of havoc.

The whole lack-of-personal-responsibility thing is very pervasive. It is all around us.

People blame their lovers, workmates, or other people in traffic for putting them in a "bad mood." Something happens on the way to work and they feel annoyed about it all day. They walk around feeling blameless, thinking about how this other person ruined everything. Well, guess what? As long as you think that way, you are not in control of your life. You are at the mercy of those around you, and that is rubbish. It's not true at all. In every situation, you choose how you react. You can choose to have your day ruined, or you can choose to laugh it off and pay attention to something which is actually important!

Eleanor Roosevelt once said, "No one can make you feel inferior without your consent", and it applies to everything in your life, not just inferiority. People have their own issues, problems, and troubles, but whether you take them on or not, and whether you let them affect you personally or not, is entirely up to you. It is your choice, and is not being forced on you! Let other people's stuff be their stuff. Let it pass you by as if it had nothing to do with you, because the truth is, it doesn't!

Some of this is quite scary. It might even make you feel afraid of your own mind. Don't be. Taking responsibility for yourself is so incredibly liberating, because it will show you the strength of your inner power. Look at all the things around you, good and not-so-good. You have attracted them into your life, whether you believe it or not. Just think, if you can create awful things for yourself -- like horrible relationships, crappy jobs, and a general sense of apathy -- what could you create if you focused your attention in a different way? What if, instead of thinking about how bad everything is all the time, you thought about how WONDERFUL life is? Because even if you look around and see things which make you unhappy, surely you must acknowledge that the world is full of marvellous things too. There's love, music, and art, delicious food and springy green grass, snowflakes and puppy kisses, hula hooping in the sunshine and exploring new cities. There are fresh vegetables and false eyelashes, majestic mountains and enormous elephants, dreams and adrenaline, sky-diving and gardening.

Life is a self-fulfilling prophecy. Whatever you think about, and whatever you expect, you will attract.

Know this now: you can spin your life into whatever you want. I say this with absolute certainty because I have done it, and so have all of my closest friends! Think about the people you admire, who live what appear to be charmed lives. How do you think they got there? Was it a series of coincidences? Are they just "lucky"? Were they fated to be that way from birth? No, no, no. They live like that because they designed it that way!

To be clear, taking responsibility for your life does not mean that any sexual abuse or violence you may have experienced are your fault. I don't know you, and I don't know your story, but what I know for sure is that no one asks for that. You may have been a victim at the time, but it is crucial to our personal evolution that we don't cling to that identity of victimhood. When I say take responsibility, what I mean is to get clear about what happened in your past, and learn how to heal from it. Otherwise, you may find yourself repeating childhood traumas you were not responsible for by manifesting them in adult life until you get really clear and conscious.

Let's begin to take responsibility for everything from this moment on. Otherwise, along your path to live the life you really want, when things don't go the way you'd prefer, you won't consider making any changes, because it won't be "your fault." It was someone else's screw-up, or it was bad weather, or the economy wasn't right. You will never make any progress that way, and you will never learn anything that way.

Even the things you experienced today -- whether you missed the bus or laughed with your lover, forgot your lunch or had a cute exchange with your favourite barista -- were all creations of your subconscious mind.

Remember that: they come from your subconscious mind. People don't set out to make their lives difficult on purpose, but our subconscious mind feeds on the things you put into your consciousness. The thoughts you think, the words you say, the music you listen to, the people you talk to, and even the blogs you read assist in creating your life! All of these things paint a picture of your future. So what is your daily routine setting you up for?

HOW TO INFUSE YOUR DAY WITH MAGIC

You have the power to set your day up any way you like, and you should do what makes you happiest! You should start as you mean to go on, after all, so why not begin the day in a way that makes you smile and makes you feel good?

Do you battle with a shrill alarm clock before you even get out of bed? That's no way to begin your day! Leave your curtains open a little bit and start waking up with the sunrise, or set your favourite song as your wake-up call. Get up 15 minutes earlier and meditate while the house is quiet, devote yourself to a few minutes of writing down the dreams you just had, or even list out your hopes for the day. Go for a run before you get in the shower, do some sun salutations when you roll out of bed, or make yourself an amazing breakfast of fresh fruit. You should incorporate whatever you think would make your day more enjoyable: start planning today, and start tomorrow!

Want some ideas? Anna Wintour, infamous Vogue editrix, wakes up every morning at 5am, and plays tennis before going into work and doing battle with the fashion elite. Richard Simmons says, "When I wake up in the morning, it's like the red curtain goes up... I twirl around the room. I thank God for the day. I fluff my hair and yell, 'GO GET 'EM, RICHARD!'" Trelise Cooper is one of New Zealand's most influential fashion designers. She employs 75 staff, and every morning at 9.15, they all gather for the ritual lighting of candles and incense, as well as five minutes of music and inspirational readings to get them ready for the day. So you see, you can make your morning as regimented or extravagant as you like, and it should be the way you like it, since it will set the tone for the rest of the day.

Most of us have a daily routine that we are used to. That can be great, because it helps us be more productive and keep our lives in order, but on the flipside, routines can be so dreadfully boring. When you think about your everyday routine, how does it sit with you? Do you feel good about it, or could it use a shake-up? Most people wake up, stumble out the door, sit in an office for eight hours, come home, eat dinner, watch television and pass out. That is not living! Where is the magic? Where is the wonder?

Here are some ideas you might like to use, expand or develop!

♥ Make lunch into an event rather than a chore. See a friend, go for a walk, or do something in your lunch-time that makes you really happy.

♥ Throw a fabulous dinner parties every month. Have everyone bring a plate, so it doesn't cost a bomb!

♥ Get really dressed up at least a few times a week. When you are well dressed, wonderfully groomed and fabulously coiffed, you will feel so much better about yourself, your day and the possibilities within it. It will give you the confidence to do new things. It is absolutely worth the extra effort!

♥ Plan amazing holidays, getaways and road-trips: you'll have something to get really excited about!

♥ Start taking a class which fascinates you.

♥ Only use heart-shaped Post It notes!

♥ Buy helium balloons which match your outfit.

♥ Sing to your plants.

♥ Change your voicemail message to something funny, silly or just ridiculous!

♥ If you feel awkward next time you go out dancing -- like you don't look good, you don't dance well enough, or you're not cool enough to be there -- take a break. Go to the corner of the room, drink some water, survey the scene and make a decision. Decide to own yourself and what you're doing. Own your dancing, own your body, take control. Decide that you're sexy, amazing, cool and glamorous. Decide that you're a fabulous dancer and that you're just going to cut loose. Decide that you're the queen (or king) of the room and that everyone else in there is just your loyal subject, dancing for your entertainment. Imagine you are wearing a crown (or put on a tiara if you feel inclined!). Don't feel the need to dance a certain way: just be you. Claim a place on the dance floor, flick your hair, spin around, and keep your head up. You have to own it. As soon as you act like you belong to be there, you'll start to have much more fun and people's reactions will mirror that back at you. Plus, there's nothing more appealing than a confident person having fun on the dance floor!

♥ Go adventuring in your city.

♥ Wake up super-early and photograph the sunrise. Plus, being up that early gives you so much time to do all kinds of things before your day "officially" starts!

♥ Dance in elevators.

♥ Practice becoming a better kisser.

♥ Put a hyacinth on your desk. There is an old Taoist proverb which says that if you lost everything and had only two coins, you should use one to buy bread to feed your body, and the other to buy hyacinths to feed your soul. A hyacinth is a symbol of sincerity and a fabulous thing to be near!

♥ Rhyme all your emails.

♥ Make cupcakes at 3am.

♥ Buy a bubble gun.

♥ Wear a sparkly bikini top under your clothing. No one else needs to know, but you will have shimmering ta-tas!

♥ Listen to lullabies before you go to sleep.

♥ Have a midnight snack date.

♥ Wear silver glitter hairspray. It's fun to go totally overboard and make your hair look like the aftermath of a fairy orgy!

You will soon find that even the smallest additions or switch-ups to your routine will make a big impact. It's really about breaking us out of the monotony that some of us are used to. Even little things like changing where you eat lunch or the way you get to work in the morning can add unexpected pleasure to a day that would have been just average if we had only stuck to what we knew.

✳ ✳ ✳

BE GOOD TO YOURSELF

Do you ever feel guilty or say bad things about yourself? Are you unable to give or receive a compliment? Do you ever feel jealous? Are you unable to give or accept affection? Do you criticise others or compare yourself with others? Are you sick all the time? Do you not take your own needs into account, not ask for what you want, or deny yourself things that you want? How many of these do you answer yes to? If you said yes even once, you could definitely up the radical self love factor in your own life!

Our overall state of happiness is essentially a reflection of how we feel about ourselves. Radical self love is the root of all of this, and if you don't have that, everything else will fall apart.

♥ Let people know how you want to be treated. This is easy to do: if you treat yourself and others well, people will notice and mirror that back at you! Or you could always just learn to ask for what you want!

♥ Learn to accept compliments. Even if you feel awkward about being told you're beautiful, intelligent, or wonderful, say thank you!

♥ Start to dish out compliments with gusto! It is one of the easiest ways for us to feel good about ourselves, and you will make someone else feel fabulous too.

♥ Learn to experience pleasure without guilt. This can take time but is absolutely worth working on.

♥ Always say good things about yourself. The old adage is true: if you don't have anything nice to say (about yourself), don't say anything at all!

♥ Be good to your body. Eat nutritious food, exercise, take care of your skin, wear clothing that makes you happy.

♥ Realise that what you DO is not who you ARE. Everyone makes mistakes, so don't get confused and tangle them up with your self-worth.

♥ Spend time around people who make you feel good.

♥ Congratulate yourself when you do well at something! This will help reinforce the fact that you don't need anyone else's approval or external validation.

♥ Use affirmations.

♥ Always visualise how you want to be, not how you are right now, and you will find yourself gravitating towards those attributes, and becoming that person. This sounds so simple, but works like nothing else!

❋ ❋ ❋

THE LANGUAGE OF CREATION

The words that we say create our reality. This is an indisputable fact. It is for this precise reason that we should concentrate on saying things which empower us, rather than making us feel bad about ourselves. We can use positive words, compliment others and ourselves, talk about the beauty of the world around us, and say how fortunate we feel to be having these experiences... or we can use negative words, criticise others, tell ourselves how unworthy we are of anything good, complain about the events of our lives, and grizzle at every given opportunity. It is just common sense to know that doing the latter is not going to make us feel good or happy in any way!

Every happy thought brings something good to you, while each negative one pushes good things away. This can be an overwhelming concept. When people first hear this and start to actively pay attention to their thoughts, they feel like they might go crazy!

Don't worry: it is totally normal to think, 'Oh God, I think so many negative thoughts and so few positive ones -- I am never going to beat this!' The good news is that positive thoughts are so much more powerful than negative ones! Even if you have been thinking negatively your entire life, it's okay. You can now begin to incorporate happy, exciting, wonderful thoughts into your daily routine to bring in oodles of positive change!

Something else to consider is that when you talk about a problem, you're watering its roots. The problem just gets stronger and more pervasive! This is not to say that we should deny that there is a problem, just that ceaselessly banging on is extremely counterproductive. People can moan about things for years without ever taking any action, and many of us insist on complaining to someone who categorically cannot do anything about the situation at hand! For example, we whine to our boyfriend about our boss, or to our best friend about our boyfriend... We need to make a practice of speaking to the person who can make a difference! Ultimately though, the key is to take action while continuing to think positively about it! Think about what you want to happen, while being proactive, and you will see magnificent results. It can be easy to dwell and get laden down with fear, but it doesn't do any good. Simply remember that you always have the choice between a happy thought and an unhappy thought. Keep your chin up and be optimistic!

Words filter into our subconscious and form the basis of the stories we tell ourselves. Be choosy about what you say, and you'll discover that there are some words we could do without. One word that really grinds my gears is "try". The word "try" indicates that we are not really in control. If we say we will try to be on time, or try to do a good job, it means nothing. Maybe we'll succeed, maybe we won't. Why even bother uttering it? We could remove "try" from our vocabulary, and our lives would have much more purpose. Doesn't it feel so much better to say "I will be on time" or "I will do a good job"? In addition to making us feel more powerful, it also gives our mind a strong message, which is one of success.

Another word which falls into this category is "can't". The word "can't" indicates that there is some obstacle. Most obstacles are created by our own mind. Why not replace it with "won't"? It is more honest! Instead of saying, "I can't clean the house", why not just say, "I won't clean the house"?!

You get the idea!

Another way to draw great things to yourself and make a change for the better is to begin using affirmations. An affirmation is a phrase that reinforces positive beliefs or behaviours. The best ones are a statement of what we want, rather than what we don't want -- remember that we attract whatever it is we think about most! -- and are phrased in the present moment.

Affirmations are extremely powerful, and they were brought into the mainstream by Louise L. Hay with her fantastic book You Can Heal Your Life. My mother has been using affirmations for years and they really work for her. I remember years ago when I was going through a rough patch, she sent me an email full of affirmations. I printed it out and taped it next to my bed. Even though at the time I was too jaded and cynical to actually say them out loud, I read them every morning and night, and I think they soaked in. They certainly helped me get to a place where I was ready to start trying to change.

For example, my new favourite affirmation is from Louise L. Hay, affirmation queen! All you have to do is say, "I am open and receptive to all good." Oooh yes! Doesn't that feel amazing?!

There is a trick to creating powerful affirmations. As much as we like to think we are ruled by our intellect, we're not: we are -- and always will be -- ruled by our emotions. There is no point in saying something -- for example, "I am a famous actress!" -- when, in your head, you're saying, 'Oh my God, I'm a failure, how am I going to pay the bills this week?' What you are feeling on the inside is always going to prevail.

To get around this, don't say affirmations that feel like an outright lie. Instead, say something that feels true for you in this moment, like, "I'm discovering my inner superstar." Starting your affirmation with "I'm discovering", "I'm becoming", or "I'm realising" will make the phrase much more palatable and believable. It will be assimilated much more quickly.

Start with one of the affirmations below, and eventually work your way up to writing your own. Write them on a piece of paper that you keep with you all the time, or stick it up somewhere in your house where you will see it constantly. Whenever you see it, say it out loud! Say them with passion and purpose. Repetition is important too, because the words will sink into your subconscious mind where they can begin to take root and have a strong effect.

Say your affirmations regularly, as often as you remember. Even work them into your daily routine -- say them as you put on your make-up in the morning, or while you exercise, or as you walk the dog. Make them as integral a part of your life as eating or breathing, and you will see wonderful results.

The most important thing to remember is that in order to make affirmations work, you need to use words that assist you in generating positive feelings. To get a bit metaphysical on you, the universe doesn't speak English, it simply reflects our feelings back at us. So whatever you say, you need to feel it all the way to your core. If you were in the process of discovering your inner superstar, how would you feel? Elated, happy, confident, powerful? Concentrate on those emotions as you say your affirmations. Allow them to build up inside you, so that they are so strong and powerful that they make you feel like you're going to combust. The more that you can really feel that feeling, the faster you will draw in the results you're hoping for.

You can use affirmations in all areas of your life, from health to love and prosperity, from careers and creativity to forgiveness or self-esteem. Here are some examples you might like to use!

❤ I love you. (This one is best used in front of the mirror!)

❤ I am discovering work that makes me feel fulfilled.

❤ Love is around every corner and joy fills my entire world.

♥ I now deserve love, romance and excitement.

♥ I am in a joyous intimate relationship with someone who really loves me.

♥ I am very thankful for all the love in my life.

♥ I can do it!

♥ I am discovering new ways to improve my health.

♥ I respect myself.

♥ I take loving care of my body now.

♥ I return my body to optimal health by giving it what it needs on every level.

♥ I am divinely guided and protected at all times.

♥ I claim my own power.

♥ I give myself the gift of freedom from the past.

♥ I am ready to be healed.

♥ As I forgive myself, it becomes easier to forgive others.

♥ I forgive myself for not being perfect, I am living the best way I know how.

♥ I am discovering how to become prosperous.

♥ I am deeply appreciated.

❤ I am now willing to be open to the immense abundance of the universe.

❤ Each day brings wonderful new surprises!

❤ I am realising that I deserve the best.

❤ I am releasing all resistance to expressing my creativity fully.

❤ My potential is unlimited.

❤ Ideas come to me easily and effortlessly.

If saying affirmations to yourself is challenging, or makes you feel ridiculous, imagine someone you love saying them to you instead. It can feel a little bit less embarrassing, and help you to get started.

Begin to pay attention to what you say and the messages you send to yourself and the people around you. It is more important than you could ever imagine!

* * *

SURROUNDING YOURSELF WITH POSITIVE PEOPLE

One thing you will quickly learn on your journey towards radical self love is that as you start to evolve, the people you have known for a long time may not "fit" anymore. This is because when you decide to place a priority on your happiness, you will begin changing, and some people will find that hard to swallow. Hopefully, most of your friends and family will be immensely supportive of this growth, but some will not, and that can be painful. It's hard to predict who will be delighted for you and who won't, and often you will be surprised by who sticks beside you, but this is all part of the progression. It is part of the evolution. While this may hurt your feelings, the unfolding of your relationships doesn't have to be ugly. Everything changes, and old things fall away to make room for the new.

It is simply a fact of life that as you become more joyous and optimistic, the friendships you have with people who can't hang with that will change. You won't make time for one another anymore, you'll find the time you spend together feels forced, or you'll just stop communicating altogether. There is nothing wrong with this, and even though it may feel uncomfortable or unfamiliar, this change will actually make your life feel more expansive. Nature abhors a vacuum, after all, and once those people are no longer part of your life, you will begin to attract people who are more in sync with you. You'll start to meet people who are more motivated, positive, excitable and full of glee. Like attracts like, after all!

When I was miserable, I attracted miserable people into my life. We would be sad, dramatic, or angry together, and because that was all I knew, it was okay. I even enjoyed it. But as I evolved, made the decision to be happy, and decided to get in control of my life once and for all, those friendships came to a standstill. We no longer shared any common interests. It was okay though, because as this happened, I started meeting new people who inspired me, encouraged me, and made me feel really good about myself.

Unfortunately, negative people are everywhere. Sometimes they are easy to spot: mean, cruel, rude and angry. But sometimes it's a little bit more subtle, and you might not even really notice it straight away. Maybe they complain all the time, maybe they discourage you from doing anything positive, perhaps their generally pessimistic attitude just makes you feel bad about yourself and life in general.

As a general rule, you can divide people into two groups: people who make you feel good, and people who don't. Hold onto the people who make you feel wonderful with both hands, and let go of anyone who makes you feel otherwise. You don't need them, you really don't!

No one has the right to be a part of your life: you get to pick and choose. Why should you let someone into your life if all they are going to do is make a mess of it? As you have probably already noticed, we are all quite capable of making glorious messes on our own, and we don't need anyone else lending a hand!

One thing I've learned over the years is that we can never change people, we can only change how we respond to them. So if your boss is miserable or your sister is rude, instead of reliving the old pattern you have with them, try reacting differently. This will totally throw them off, and will completely change your dynamic. If you don't believe me, try it yourself!

Sometimes though, those negative people can be hard to shake; they can even be members of our family. It can hurt to realise that someone close to us is not as supportive as we wish they were. It's hard to deal with the fact that our mothers, fathers, sisters, brothers, aunts, and uncles can't pull it together and be happy for us.

Family is important, sure, but when people use "family" as an excuse to treat one another badly, you have to wonder what it's all worth. I have a lot of friends who have chosen to extricate themselves from the family they were born into, and have created their own families, either by marrying, having or adopting children, or by gathering friends who they really love and cherish. These people often seem happier -- and more well-adjusted! -- than anyone else.

This is not to say that you should cut your mother out of your life for trivial reasons, but if, after years, she cannot help but be negative and destructive, you might find that your life is a lot better without her in it. This goes double, triple, even quadruple if your family is abusive in any way. You are better than that shit.

Breaking contact with a member of your family can be difficult, and there is no real recipe for guaranteed success, since every situation is totally different. That having been said, if this is something you want to do, the most important thing is that you know what you'd like your desired outcome to be. Once you have made up your mind, it will begin to become clear to you what you should do next. This is not to say the process will be easy, but once you have severed the connection, you will feel like you have regained control of your life.

When someone in our family says something to us which we find hard to swallow, it can hurt much more than words from some idle stranger. Be strong. Only your opinion of yourself matters. Tell yourself this over and over again, and it will begin to become true for you.

✱ ✱ ✱

YOU CANNOT LET PEOPLE DEFEAT YOU

Other people will always have opinions about you, your life, and what you do with it. Some of their opinions will be positive and congratulatory, some of them will be negative, and a few will be downright nasty. This is just a fact of life. Regardless of how much love you surround yourself with, and the amount of love you put out into the universe, people are always going to have an opinion on you and what you're up to. Some of them will even have the gall to share their thoughts with you, as if it will somehow change you!

Most of the time we can take this stuff with a grain of salt, and laugh it off. After all, 99% of opinions are ridiculous at best. But sometimes they bother us, upset us, or just make us want to punch something!

It can be so hard to take a compliment, and yet, we're so quick to believe people's criticism. Most of us will remember a compliment for a few minutes, but can recall insults for YEARS! Unfortunately, it is just how our brains are wired, all part of our negativity bias. We would be much happier if we could simply let it go, and so that is something we should work towards.

Why would you take someone else's opinion more seriously than your own? Why does their opinion hold more weight than yours? They are not living your life, you are, and therefore it is completely inconsequential. Think about it in reverse. If you told Angelina Jolie you thought she was a terrible actress, would you expect her to laugh it off? Or would you expect her to have a crisis of faith? I'd think it's likely she'd laugh and walk away, unaffected.

It can take years for us to really stop caring what people think or say about us. The story goes that as you age, you care less about other people's opinions of you. We are supposed to feel more comfortable with ourselves in our mid-thirties, and as we feel more comfortable in our own skin, we worry less about what people may or may not think. But what if you're 14 years old and the opinions your classmates have of you seems to be ruining your life? As with anything which typically takes "years", I like to tap to speed up the process. (Nothing has to take years unless you want it to!)

We all want to be liked and it can hurt when people seem to have it in for us. Beyond tapping, all you can do is decide not to worry about it, and continue doing what you do.

You absolutely cannot let other people and their thoughts get the better of you. Decide that it is not an option! If all the great people in the world listened to -- and took the advice of -- their critics, the world would be nowhere near as wild, fabulous and diverse as it is.

Dale Carnegie used to say that unjust criticism was a disguised compliment, because it meant that you had made someone jealous or envious. He gave the example that no one ever kicks a dead dog, so next time you are faced with criticism, keep this in mind!

✳ ✳ ✳

HOW TO SET AMAZING GOALS

To put it simply, happiness will elude you unless you have a goal. You need to know where you want to go and what you want to do in life, and goals will provide you with an essential roadmap. Without this information, you'll be lost, adrift.

I learned about goal-setting from my father, and it's one of the most valuable things he ever taught me. Here are some of my top tips.

♥ Think big. If you don't know where to begin, or you feel like you have absolutely no ambition, take some time out for yourself and just allow your mind to wander. Give yourself permission to dream. Get somewhere comfortable and drift away on your imagination.

What kind of lifestyle have you always wished you had? Would you like to live in a hippie commune in San Francisco, or is a brownstone in New York more your style? How about volunteering in India, or owning a fleet of cruise ships? Have you always wanted to run away and join the circus, or would you like to start a community kitchen where people can eat wonderfully hearty but inexpensive meals? Picture everything that would surround that lifestyle. Would you drive a car or ride a moped? Would your bedroom be like a Moroccan retreat or would it be minimal and zen? Would you have a husband, wife, lover, girlfriend, boyfriend, harem or keep to yourself? Would you have any pets? How often would your friends visit? What kind of friends would you like? Witty, urbane, comfortable, sweet?

Grab a piece of paper and start scribbling down ideas. Don't judge yourself while you write. Just because you're writing something down doesn't mean you have to go out and do it; just give yourself some options. Then narrow it down to things that really turn your crank.

♥ How will you know you have succeeded? The best way to set a goal is to define success as what/how many/how much by a certain date. For example, "Get famous" isn't a real, achievable goal, because there's no way to measure it. How will you know that you're famous? On the other hand, "Be on the cover of Rolling Stone in 2020" is a great goal because it's measurable. On December 31st 2020, if you haven't achieved it, you'll know. So, pick a time frame, and put a stake in the ground.

♥ Set a goal that scares you! If your goals are boring, your life is going to be incredibly dull. Goals should feel like a stretch, they should make you nervous! Come up with something that terrifies you! Set a goal that makes you gulp as you write it down. How about something like, "Move to Austria by November" or "Start my own business and leave my boring office job within two years"? FEAR! Tremble! Quake in your boots! Your goal will swell in your brain, absorb a whole lot of your brain power, scare the hell out of you... and then start happening. Even better!

♥ Write it down. Unless you write your goal down, it's just an idle thought -- and unless you review and re-read your goals regularly, you'll forget them. Grab a big sheet of paper, write your goals nice and big, and then pin it to the wall. You can also try writing your main goal on a small piece of paper and tucking it into a clear pocket in your wallet so you see it all the time. The closer your goal is to the front of your mind, the better.

♥ Break your goals into chunks. If you want to be an Olympic athlete, you don't just turn up and hope to qualify. Years of work go into it first. For example, if you want to write a book, you need to pick a subject, outline your chapters, write multiple drafts, find an editor, hire a designer, and the list goes on. Think in steps: it will make your objective seem much more manageable, and will help keep you from feeling defeated or overwhelmed. For each goal, use a fresh piece of paper and write down each step. When you complete an action, mark it off with a big tick. It's vital to celebrate the small triumphs along the way!

♥ Visualise what you want, and make your goal as real as you can. Let's use the previous example of getting on the cover of Rolling Stone: why not make a mock-up of the magazine with your face on the front? Or maybe you want to visit New York. Cut out a picture of yourself and stick it onto a photo of Central Park! Take a screen capture of one of the places you want to go, and then make it your desktop wallpaper, so you see it every day. I have heard of people who write themselves million dollar cheques and stick them on the ceiling above their bed... and it works!

♥ Act "as if". One of the best ways to achieve something, strange as it may sound, is to pretend it has already happened. Let's say your distant goal is to be a publishing magnate. How different would your life be if you managed to achieve that? Okay, now remove all the material things that would change (better car, huge house, office with a view of the city), and think about how you would behave if you were a publishing big-shot. Odds are, your posture would be different from how it is today. You might not slob around in the house in a pair of moccasins all day, either! You'd probably wake up early, exercise and get into your day. You'd be comfortable with your success and not threatened by other people, so you would ask for what you wanted and tell people if they weren't delivering what you expected. You'd be polite and charming and charismatic and happy to do favours for others. Start acting that way today. It will prove that you are serious about your goal, and you will start to attract the right people and opportunities to make your dreams a reality.

♥ Don't fear obstacles. When you're trying to achieve something, obstacles are inevitable. Instead of being frustrated or angry or feeling like the world is against you, just see it as a test of your passion and drive. You need to get over the hump and prove that you want something; that you're hungry for it. There are always going to be little things that don't go your way, or people who don't have your vision. That's okay... just stay the course. Think about people who have achieved amazing things and consider how they'd deal with it. Odds are good that they would pout for about a second, and then just get on with it.

♥ Ask for help and watch other people. Don't be afraid to ask other people for assistance. Most people are thrilled to do it, as long as you make it worth their while. Be vocal about how appreciative you are, buy them a really excellent dinner, or give them a bottle of fantastic wine! The other thing to keep in mind is that whatever you're trying to achieve has probably been done before. This is not to dissuade you, of course: it's to make you see that it can be done, and that you should watch whoever achieved it before you! Maybe they wrote a book about how they did it, maybe they spoke about it in an interview, or perhaps they even made a movie about it. Take all these things and learn from them.

Anthony Robbins says, "Success leaves clues". Don't try and reinvent the wheel unless you can help it. Use other people's experiences to bolster your own.

♥ Always persist. Start now! Your greatest asset is this day, right now, right here. There is no better time to start turning your life around, and manifesting whatever it is you want. It is never too late: you always have today. Start IMMEDIATELY!

WEAPONS IN THE FIGHT AGAINST SAD

Here are some more ideas to keep you buoyant in times of trouble!

♥ Use essential oils. The effect of scent on our emotions is major, and a lot of us totally underrate it. You can dot essential oils onto a tissue, use in an oil burner, or even add them to your food or drink to boost your mood! Some of the best oils to use to make you happy are lavender, orange, rose, ylang ylang, lemon, jasmine, coriander, clove bud, cinnamon, petitgrain, roman chamomile, bergamot, geranium, frankincense and ginger. All of these oils have their own unique attributes, so do a bit of Googling to find out which is best for your particular situation! For example, lavender is great for relaxation (and restful sleep), jasmine calms people down while also acting as an aphrodisiac, and lemon is great for lifting spirits, as well as helping you concentrate. Essential oils are really amazing and can be used so many different ways, so have a look into them. You will be amazed by what you learn!

♥ Eat more chocolate. Put simply, it makes people feel good. Chocolate is a natural analgesic, which is a pain-killer. It also releases endorphins into your system, and endorphins are the chemical which makes us feel happy and peaceful. Some researchers have said that chocolate contains teeny tiny amounts of the same chemicals found in marijuana, which could be why it makes us feel so blissed out when we eat it! Chocolate is very high in magnesium, so often a chocolate craving is a sign that we need more magnesium in our diet. However, most commercial candy bars are absolutely loaded with artificial crap, so the more pure the chocolate, the better! I love raw chocolate for this reason, and it's so rich you'll only need a couple of squares. Raw chocolate gives you a high like no other!

♥ Eat chilli peppers! When you eat hot peppers, your brain releases endorphins, which make you feel awesome. Develop an appreciation for spicy foods!

♥ Exercise. We all know that this is something that we are supposed to do, but beyond being good for body, it's great for your brain! In fact, it is one of the very best ways to boost your mood. In clinical trials, exercise has been proven to be as effective at combatting depression as medication or cognitive therapy! Now that is amazing.

♥ Smile more often. As well as being scientifically proven that smiling actually makes you happy, it also makes you more attractive to other people and therefore more likely that they will a) smile back, b) want to be your friend, c) want to be your lover! It even works when you're not feeling good: one of the very best ways to fix a rotten mood is to manipulate your mouth muscles into a little grin! As I said earlier, our physiology -- what we do with our bodies -- informs our psychology -- how we feel -- so if you stand up straight and smile, you'll miraculously start to feel happier.

♥ Laugh! It's one of the best ways to get happy quickly. If you don't feel like laughing, fire up Youtube and watch clips of your favourite comedian. There are even laughter yoga gatherings in many cities, where people congregate in parks and simply laugh!

♥ Get organised! It's so hard to be happy when you never know what's coming next. If you can get your life in order a little bit -- for example, by paying your bills in advance, or planning out your week and knowing what needs to be done -- you'll have much less information to hold in your head, which makes more space for joy. Clear out all the banal things, and put them down on paper, so that you don't really have to think about them anymore. That's just one of the reasons why I write everything down. It keeps everything straight so I don't have to worry about it. It makes a huge difference.

♥ Engage in some heavy-duty pampering. When I've had a long week and feel kind of exhausted, one of the best ways I know to deal with it is to go to my favourite spa and get a pedicure. It gives me an opportunity to zone out, relax, and have someone else look after me for a little while.

❤ Listen to music. There is almost nothing better than listening to some of my favourite tunes. When I'm happy, music serves to elevate my mood even further, but when I'm not, it helps me feel better. It's not just a coincidence, either. While some of it is psychological (like music you associate with a certain person or positive memory), much of it is physiological. Music relieves stress, relaxes the body, can remove pain, and even stop anxiety! It slows down your breathing and heart rate, because music calms down the cells and tissues in your body, in turn relaxing the lungs. It even helps your heart. Music causes the tissue in the inner lining of blood vessels to dilate (or expand) in order to increase blood flow. If in doubt, blast your favourite song!

❤ Lose yourself in art. Go to galleries, read books, attend the ballet -- do something which reminds you that there is so much beauty outside yourself!

❤ Be grateful for what you have. Reminding yourself of all the good things in your life is an immensely powerful way to turn your mood around. On my site, I make my gratitude lists public every Thursday (the feature is called Things I Love Thursday, and I've been running it since 2007!). Doing this helps keep me aware of the multitude of things in my life which are wonderful, because as we all know, it can be very easy to forget! I recommend writing weekly -- or even daily -- gratitude lists. You might think it's so simple it couldn't possibly work, but if you give it a try, you'll realise how effective it is!

❤ Make the choice to be happy. Life is never perfect, and it never will be, but we can decide to be happy right now, in this moment, anyway. If you are always waiting for things to fall into place, or you are constantly thinking, 'Oh, I'll be happy when...', happiness will always elude you. Often, the amount of unhappiness we feel is the distance between how good we think our lives are, and how good we think they should be. Happiness is a choice, and you have to decide to be happy regardless of everything else.

The marvellous thing about happiness is that in a lot of ways, it's very easy. You can either choose a thought which makes you happy, or a thought that makes you anxious, and you can make that choice every moment of every day.

#RSLBOOK

HOMEWORK

_ _ _

♥ **DECIDE TO TAKE RESPONSIBILITY FOR YOUR LIFE.**

From this day forward, practice thinking differently by taking responsibility for everything that happens to you. Ask yourself, how could I have manifested another outcome?

♥ **COME UP WITH NEW WAYS TO MAKE YOUR DAILY ROUTINE MORE MAGICAL.**

Begin to incorporate a couple of new ones each week. If they make you feel happier, great! If not, discard and try something new.

♥ **START USING AFFIRMATIONS.**

Begin with a few from this chapter, and as you become more comfortable, create your own. Write them on your mirror or window using a whiteboard pen. Let the positive words sink into your subconscious and lift you up!

♥ **INVESTIGATE SOME OF THE 'WEAPONS IN THE FIGHT AGAINST SAD'.**

See which work best for you! When you find activities or solutions that resonate, write them down somewhere. My suggestion? Start keeping a Radical Self Love Bible, which is a notebook full of affirmations, power thoughts, big dreams, and lists of things to do when you're feeling discouraged.

♥ **KNOW THAT WHAT YOU DO TODAY IS IMPORTANT.**

In fact, what you do every day is important! As I said at the beginning of the chapter, all we have is this moment, and it is ours to do with as we wish. You can be happy or sad. You can change your habits, or you can be who you always were. You can live a life of wonder, magic, excitement, and adventure, or you can live a life which is hard, boring, monotonous, and difficult. You have always been in charge, and today is no different. In the words of Maya Angelou, "Life loves to be taken by the lapel and told 'I'm with you kid. Let's go'."

LOVE, SEX, THE GALAXY AND EVERYTHING

From falling in love to
co-habitation, and all the beauty
and madness contained within!

Falling in love is easy: it happens, all across the world, every minute of every day. Eyes lock across a crowded market, or you pass someone who makes your head swivel. It's trivial to find someone who piques your interest, but finding the person who is right for you? That's a much taller order.

Relationships can be tricky. Some of us seem to be searching forever, while others appear to meet a soulmate on every corner. Why do some people have all the luck, while the rest of us are left floundering?

Let's take it way back (to Chapter One). Intimate relationships should always come secondary to your relationship with yourself, and -- like it or lump it -- will always be directly impacted by how much you love yourself. If you don't think you're a badass babe, you'll always be looking for someone to complete you or fill an emotional hole. (Spoiler alert: this doesn't work!)

The best relationships happen when you combine two people who have their self-respect on lock. To put it simply, you gotta be in love with your wonderful self. You should be able to look in the mirror, pout, flick your hair, wink at yourself and think, 'Babe, you are divine.'

Now, before you start thinking you'll never get to that point, take a breath. It takes time to get there, and loving yourself is not a destination, it is a journey. We all have down days where our skin sucks, none of our clothing fits, and our brain doesn't seem to be working. But if you can make kissy faces at yourself in the mirror and put on hot pink lipstick even when you're not feeling it, you're doing a damn good job.

The other option -- lovers who don't love themselves -- is a losing game, like playing tennis with a hand grenade. If you keep hitting it back and forth, someone's going to lose an eye! It just doesn't work. You'll need your partner to prop up your self-esteem (since you can't do it yourself), or you'll feel insecure, and become convinced your boyfriend is going to leave you for someone else (and then, since life is a self-fulfilling prophecy, they probably will). Maybe you'll think your girlfriend is too good for you, so you'll self-sabotage... And maybe because, deep down, you think you're unworthy of a great person's attention, you'll settle for someone who is kind of a jerk.

Clearly, none of these scenarios are the Hollywood ending we're all hoping for!

A relationship should be like an explosion of awesomeness. You should both be contributing your own unique brand of marvellousness, and when your powers are combined, you should both increase in brightness and radiance like a goddamn supernova. Together, you are stronger, smarter, braver, and more awesome than ever before.

Of course, you will have your bad days, your fights, your squabbles, your disagreements over who should do the dishes tonight. But the most crucial thing is that there needs to be a balance, and some give-and-take. You don't want to date someone whose unhappiness casts a shadow over your entire life, and you don't want to be a weight around your partner's ankle, holding them back from achieving their optimal potential. That is not the point of a relationship! You both need to be adding something to one another's lives that you wouldn't have otherwise.

Why be in a relationship if it doesn't make you happier? If it doesn't make you a better person, why are you wasting your time?

We can probably all agree that happiness is a major goal of being in a relationship with someone else, but the rest of it is up to you. We all have different expectations -- some of which we may have learned from watching our parents, some of which we will have concluded on our own -- so I can't tell you what you should be looking for in an ideal relationship. I can only talk about my own desires!

It's for this reason that I recommend giving this a little thought. I'm a big fan of list magic, maybe because it appeals to the Virgo in me. What is list magic? It's exactly what it sounds like: you simply sit down and make a list of the things you want.

This works brilliantly for relationships. As well as helping you to gain some major clarity and perspective, it's also a great thing to have around when you fall for some fool who isn't up to scratch. Just look back at your list and see how many criteria they fulfill! It's like having a BFF with a deadly accurate point of view!

Once upon a time, when I was going through some romantic upheaval, I flipped open a notebook and started making a list of qualities I was looking for in my next serious lover. Admittedly, when I wrote it, I was thinking about someone specific, but it still holds true and is essentially my checklist of ideal attributes.

The whole subject is interesting to me, especially when you consider that we all want different things. Some of the things on my list will be things you couldn't give a flying fig about, and some things on your list would render me confused. This is just how it is, which is of course how we all end up with such vastly different people.

Relationships are so fascinating, aren't they? I often walk down the street and look at couples and wonder why they're together. Do you ever do that? I always wonder, how did they get together, and why do they stay? What does their love affair look like behind closed doors? What was it that made them fall in love? Does he make killer linguine? Is she a complete genius whom he loves having as his partner on pub trivia night? The whole thing is so weird and fantastic.

Have you ever examined your romantic patterns? If not, when you think back on the people you've dated, you'll probably notice that there are certain things they have in common.

In my case, I don't really have a "type". I've dated designers, tattoo artists, rappers, programmers, poets, and musicians, all shapes, sizes, and ethnicities, from totally diverse backgrounds. But there are a few attributes they all share. They were all able to make me laugh and did so often. They were all very intelligent, and had a unique perspective on the world. Those are still things that are important to me.

But as I've grown older and learned more about life (as well as myself), I've added a few other things into the mix. While humour and intelligence are still way, way up there, it's vital for me to be with someone who is ambitious, encourages me to be ambitious too, and -- most importantly -- has a positive outlook on life. I have dated my fair share of apathetic, negative guys in the past, and that no longer interests me (even though at the time, I was in the same place, and so it was okay by me). As we grow, we change, and as we change, what we're looking for changes too. That's one of the wonderful things about life: it's always in flux!

List magic works best when we are open-minded, and so I would advise against adding anything too superficial to your list. You need to be smart about this! Of course it would be nice, for example, to meet and fall in love with a wealthy heiress, but would you rather someone had money, or that they were trustworthy and intelligent?

The other thing about adding silly, shallow items to your list is that it massively reduces the pool of people to whom you'll give a chance. 6'5" basketball players who make seven figures aren't that easy to come by, whereas a happy, talented, cute-as-hell guy is much more obtainable.

Love happens in the most unlikely places. People meet under unusual circumstances all the time and stay together for 60 years. If you think you're only going to meet your future wife at a Yankees game or an Ivy League mixer, you're cutting out massive amounts of the population, and probably missing what is right in front of you.

Once you've written your list, you'll have clarity and know what you want, and that's excellent. Knowledge is power! But it's not all one-sided. You need to be able to give something BACK, too. Think about it: what do you bring to the table? For this reason, it's worth turning inward a little bit and asking yourself some questions.

Here are some suggestions.

What qualities are you looking for in a partner that you would benefit from developing yourself? What beliefs do you have about love and the way love works? Why do you believe this? Are these beliefs helping or hindering you? Is it time to let them go? What could you do to make yourself more lovable? (See also: how could you improve yourself for all future partners?) What steps could you take to express your love for your partner more fully? And finally, are you really and truly willing to deal with the fact that any valuable relationship will stir up the most negative facets of both partners, and call upon both of you to heal your deepest wounds?

(That last one is a knee-trembler, no? Don't worry: we'll dive deep into that question later in this chapter.)

You never really know when or how you will meet your next great love. Most of the time it just comes up and smacks you right out of the blue. My parents (who have been married for over 30 years) met when my mother walked into his shop one day, wanting to buy a stereo. They had a tumultuous first date involving wisdom teeth extraction, pasta, the request of a spoon, and, well, the rest is history!

One of the great secrets about love is that it always shows up when you're not looking for it. This might seem like a coincidence, but it's not: it's one of the core tenets of the law of attraction and manifesting. Love shows up when you're not expecting it because you have let go of your expectations, and you're not obsessing over finding the perfect person. Clinging super-tightly to your wants, needs and desires is a surefire way to block your blessings.

It always happens that way: I declare that I am officially disinterested in being in a relationship with anyone, and then, all of a sudden, I meet someone wonderful. And I'm just like everyone else: I have definitely had my phases of obsessing over someone, freaking out, and spending hours on the phone talking about it. But once I eventually get over it, relax, and realise how much fun it is to be single, I inevitably meet someone who is so cool that I can't resist jumping on in.

* * *

BEING IN A RELATIONSHIP

Love is about risk. Romance is magical and wonderful, but it's also a real stomach-churner. The rewards are enormous -- when it's good, it lights up your heart like a pinball machine -- but there are dangers, too. What if you aren't accepted when you tell the truth about who you are and what you want? What if you're as real as you can be and you get rejected? What if he cheats? What if you find out you're not the only woman in her life? All of these things can happen and more.

That's why love, the real stuff -- not the silly, I'm-here-until-someone-better-comes-along stuff -- requires bravery, courage, and strength. People who really put their hearts out there and take the chance should be awarded medals, because it's hard.

I hate to break it to you, but EVERYONE gets hurt in love. You might not necessarily get dumped or cheated on, but sometimes things don't go how you wish they would, and that hurts. When you make an emotional investment in someone and they don't return it? Yeah, that smarts. It makes you sad and angry, and pledge to swear off dazzling smiles and cute phone-calls forever. But you have to pull yourself up and move onwards, because if you don't risk anything, you risk even more.

1. Establish some rules and boundaries

I know this sounds boring and non-magical, but it's very important. For example: are you exclusive? Basic, yes, but it's vital information. I say this because of my own experiences. This is a mistake that you make once!

Once I was dating this guy -- we were pretty much boyfriend and girlfriend except we hadn't SAID as much (take note) -- and we had been seeing each other for a couple of months, talked constantly, and were all up in each other's business. Then one weekend he slept with someone else. Wait, what?! Imagine me doing a triple-take. To say I was surprised is a massive understatement!

When he told me about it, he knew he had done the wrong thing, but defended it by saying, "Oh, I didn't think we were exclusive".

If that happened today, I would see it as an enormous red flag, and not pursue the relationship any further, but I was young, and I decided to try to look past it. He apologised as many times as he could, and did his best to make it up to me. We stayed together for years, and in fact, the relationship I had with him was the longest I ever had (with the exception of my husband). But even though I loved him desperately, in my mind the power balance was always off. I felt that I had allowed him to treat me with a lack of respect, and I felt powerless and weak for having tolerated his behaviour. It was crushing for my self-esteem, and I was never really able to get over it. I'm positive it contributed to the eventual souring of our relationship.

Do as I say, not as I do (or did)!

2. Use your words!

Yes, you have probably heard this a million times, but -- other than mutual respect -- the most important thing in any relationship is communication.

Let me break this down for you so you understand exactly what I mean.

Communication means telling your lover what's going on. It means not expecting them to be able to read your mind (because they can't, even if you're dating David Copperfield). Communication means expressing any problems, asking questions, and talking about what's troubling you. It means sharing how you really feel, both positive and negative. It means being honest and open and real, even when it's awkward, even when it's a "bad time", and even when you feel like an idiot for saying out loud what's in your head. It means taking risks and opening up even when you don't want to. It means not-being-sure-if-they're-going-to-give-you-a-weird-look-when-you-say-this, but doing it anyway.

You just have to be honest. I know that can be more complicated than it sounds, and if you've ever had to have a difficult state-of-the-union type conversation, you know this. Sometimes, it might seem less vexing to just lie and act like everything is okay all the time, but that is totally destructive, dishonest, and -- let's face it -- plain old bad for you. The whole situation will become ugly and convoluted, and five months down the track you're going to EXPLODE with all the things which are driving you CRAZY and they'll kick you out of their apartment and put your phone number all over Craigslist. Save yourself 100 creepy voicemails from anonymous weirdos: just take a deep breath and talk about what's bugging you!

Having a "talk" doesn't have to be dramatic and filled with long, tension-laden pauses or theatrical stares out the window at the rain pelting the sidewalk. No, not at all. Just start talking.

A little tip: it's easier for people to have deep, emotional conversations when they're not looking at each other. You may have noticed you have great chats when you're out walking with a friend, and this is why. It's easier to be sincere and genuine when you're not face-to-face. There's less social pressure.

Truthfully, though, it doesn't matter how you get started, just as long as you get the words out, and they listen. Sometimes even when neither of you can come up with a resolution right away, you'll feel much better just having gotten the issue off your chest. It's awful to feel like you are suffering in silence; at least when you get it out, you can use both your noggins to find some sort of solution.

When someone is talking to you about something that you know is important to them, use your best active listening skills. Active listening means that you prove you are listening to them, by saying "Yes", "Uh huh", or generally agreeable noises after they make their main points, as well as repeating back to them what they've said every now and again, just to clarify that you understand. It is a great skill to have and should be practiced often. Google "active listening" for best results!

If you, like me, find it difficult to remember all the things you have to say when it's time for a serious conversation, you might find it useful to make notes. Yes, this is geeky, but it works!

Little tips

♥ If you've been together for a while, and the natural novelty is starting to wear off, it's essential to work at the magic. You should always look forward to seeing your lover, and if you're not feeling it, spend a couple of days apart! Get back together for a fun date, and break out of the rut you're in. For a lot of us, boredom is the beginning of the end, so keeping things fresh is vital!

♥ Never go to sleep angry. It's a bit of a cliché, but works for me. This is all about clearing things up quickly and not allowing time for grudges and resentments to build up. Plus, who wants to wake up pissed off because of something that happened the night before? You'll just ruin your whole day, and that is no way to go through life. Every day should be a fabulously blank slate. It's wonderful to wake up in the morning, look at your lover and give them a kiss without secretly thinking, You are so annoying and I am going to poison you tonight!

♥ Make an effort. Yes indeed: get dressed up, and maintain your personal grooming routine! While it's nice to get to that stage where you can be comfortable around your partner in a pair of ratty old sweatpants, hanging out in your dingiest, most unflattering garb is not the ideal scenario, is it? Embrace date night: go out to dinner together at least once a week, and wear your sassiest ensemble! Put in the amount of effort that you would if you were going out on a first or second date. You should respect yourself and love yourself enough to eat well, stay active, and dress nicely, and the same applies to your partner. It's a fantastic feeling to go out together, knowing you both look awesome and that you are the fun, happy couple every other twosome wants to be!

♥ Have fun together! This one is so essential. Make plans to actually do things together, otherwise it's very easy to slump into the couch every night and eat takeout before crawling into bed. That's okay sometimes, and in fact, it is desperately needed on occasion, but every night?! Come on, you can do better than that! Go to art shows, take long walks, exercise together (it triggers adrenaline and endorphins, which will bond you together as well as make you irresistibly sexy to one another), try out new restaurants, get drunk in bars and make out in public, hold hands, climb trees, go swimming, take road trips, and have a fun date at least once a week. Make it a rule to spend one night together OUT of the house! It will give you something to look forward to, and keep you smitten.

♥ Do little things for your lover, because it shows that you care and are paying attention. Help them out with something you know they've been meaning to do (like helping to clean their apartment), or buy them something they once mentioned in passing. Even giving them a massage at the end of a long day will help remind them how much you care.

✳ ✳ ✳

SEXY SEXY SEX

Don't forget to have sex! Yes, it sounds obvious, I know, but sometimes we need to be reminded. The cold hard facts are as follows: once the sex stops, you might as well just be friends, since ultimately that is really what differentiates a really close friendship from an intimate relationship.

If you're bored stiff by the sex you're having, trust me, you are not doing it right. Great sex is much, much more than just lying back and thinking of England! It requires communication (yep, that old chestnut), exploring and trying new things, reading sex books, being open to unfamiliar ideas, being vocal, and really enjoying one another! Let's be honest: anything gets a bit boring after you've done it often enough, which is why it's really important to switch it up as much as you can. Work out what you like!

Now here's the thing: some people you will have amazing chemistry with, some not so much. Often, and here's the kicker, you will have immense sexual chemistry with people you would want to murder if you were actually dating, and only so-so sexual chemistry with someone you're madly in love with. Sometimes you have to work at it, and if your socks are not being knocked off, you just have to keep at it. Try new things, ask what they want and like, tell them what you want and like, and -- crucially -- discuss it when you're not in bed together. (No one wants a performance critique while naked!)

If you don't tell them what you want or like sexually -- because you don't know, or you're too embarrassed -- your sex life may end up less interesting than what's on television. Human sexuality is fascinating and all-encompassing, so for God's sake, talk about it with your lover! Don't be shy!

If, after hearing about your kinks and curiosities, your lover thinks you're nuts, that's their problem, but did you ever consider that maybe they like the exact same thing, and are also too shy to mention it? If one of you bit the bullet and brought it up, the two of you could be in ecstasy 24/7! Nothing is that wild, really, and this world is full of people who just love freaky things. Your partner might be one of them, so let me just say once more: talk to them about it or perish!

Sometimes, it can take a while for you to really wake up to these truths. I didn't start having good sex until I was about 25 years old, and became less terrified of expressing my desires. Like the old adage goes, if you don't ask, you'll never get.

* * *

SEX TIPS FROM A LIMOUSINE DRIVER

My life has taken me to some unusual and unexpected places, and I have met my fair share of wild and wacky people. Some stand out more than others, like, for example, the limousine driver I met in Toronto, who spent our entire trip explaining how he and his wife kept their marriage -- to use his words -- "spicy".

Let's be real: at the time, I really didn't want to hear it, and it was a bit of a TMI (Too Much Information) situation. But I have to admit, he had some very salient points. He was about 50 years old, and he said that they had been happily married for a long time. Here are the tips he shared that I thought were worth passing along.

♥ MAKE SEX A PRIORITY

When you both come home from a super-long day at work, and you're exhausted and just want to lie down, don't go to bed expecting to have sex. It won't happen. Either you'll both be snoring within seconds, or one of you will pass out, and the other person will lie there in the dark feeling rejected. It's simple, really: beds make people tired and sleepy, which is why they are made for sleeping in. His point? Have sex somewhere else. He was a fan of doin' it in the closet (how very Michael Jackson), or on the couch when his kids were out. (Oh my.) But think about it: you don't have to have sex in the house! Get outside, book a hotel room, find somewhere unusual, and go crazy. It's more fun that way. Just don't get arrested; I will not be held responsible if you do!

♥ IMPOSE A MORATORIUM ON UGLY, COMFORTABLE PYJAMAS

This rule goes for both you! Ugly pyjamas really don't need to exist. You are a fox, and you don't have to wear unflattering grandma pyjamas to sleep in! You'll be just as comfortable in something silky; you don't have to wear a nest of bondage-esque webbing to seduce your main squeeze. Trust me, you'll get your money's worth! The limousine driver made a point of telling me how much he enjoyed seeing his wife in a g-string. No further comment required!

♥ MAKE "SEX DATES"

This may not sound romantic, but truly, if you want anything in this life, you need to make time for it, and most crucially, schedule it. Otherwise, you'll find yourself with a serious lack of time. My driver told me that he and his wife make sex dates, where -- yes -- they book a hotel room for a night, and make a point of getting down to business. They also go to Las Vegas once a year, where they gamble, drink, eat, and screw like mad. Having something like that on the agenda will unite you, and give you both something to look forward to. Talk about a recipe for a happy sex life!

ISSUES

Time to tear into that question from earlier. Are you really and truly willing to deal with the fact that any valuable relationship will stir up the most negative facets of both partners, and call upon both of you to heal your deepest wounds?

While it would be great if all relationships were a beautiful give-and-take between two well- balanced individuals, that is not often the case. Even the most sane, grounded, emotionally-aware couples will have problems, simply by virtue of being human and by being intimate with one another.

Relationships have issues, problems, and things that need to be worked through; this is just how it is. Sometimes your dilemmas will be small (I like to wake up early, you like to sleep in) and sometimes they will be big (I have been abused so I push you away, and you were rejected by your parents, so you don't deal well with being rejected). All relationships require work, but the important thing is that you're both willing to put in the effort and make changes to your behaviour so you can move through it together.

There's a question on OKCupid which says, "Relationships require compromise. Yours or theirs?" Ha! It's a good question, though. If you're having problems in your relationship -- like one of you doesn't feel listened to, your sex-life is lacking or you just can't stand his friends -- one person shouldn't be struggling through it alone. If it's a true partnership, you should both be equally committed to solving any troubles that come up.

One of the best things a couple can do to help strengthen their relationship is to simply start making a concerted effort to be nice to one another. This sounds obvious, but in practice, can be quite ground-breaking. I'm sure I'm not alone in utilising sarcasm and teasing my beloved as a way of showing affection, but it doesn't contribute anything positive to the relationship. In one of my more serious relationships, my boyfriend and I decided to abandon sarcasm, to stop being mean to one another in jest, and to instead say what we really meant. It's such a simple concept, but it made an incredible difference to the way we related, and brought us much closer. When we gave up sarcasm, there was never any doubt about how much we liked each other, meaning there was no insecurity or miscommunication. It's definitely something worth trying if you and lover are faux-mean to one another a lot; you'll be surprised by how much happier it will make you both.

This idea is even backed up by science. In 1994, John Gottman said there was one indicator of marital success, and that was at least a five-to-one ratio of positive to negative interactions. He said that stable marriages provide five times more instances of smiling, touching, complimenting and laughing than sarcasm, criticism and insults. (Source: Psychology: Eighth Edition; David G. Meyers) Even if you're just idly dating, it's clear that a copious amount of positive interactions will make your relationships stronger and happier.

All people are different, and sometimes, no matter how deeply two people are in love, they have trouble communicating with one another. I am a great fan of Gary Chapman's Five Love Languages. In his book, Chapman posits that there are five different ways (or "languages") we show love to others. These five languages are words of affirmation (giving compliments, saying "I love you", etc.), quality time (spending time together, doing activities as a couple), gifts (buying presents, booking a surprise trip to the Bahamas), acts of service (washing your lover's car, helping them solve a problem, cooking them dinner) and physical touch (back-rubs, make-out sessions, sex, etc.). While everyone requires all five of the "languages" for a successful relationship, people need some more than the others.

For example, I know that my two major love languages are words of affirmation and physical touch, whereas I've dated people who showed me how much they loved me by performing acts of service, or buying me gifts.

That's the problem: we show our lovers how much we like them by speaking our own love language. So when I'm busy telling my lovers how much I appreciate them, or holding their hand, that may not mean a lot to them. They might feel more loved if we just spent some time together.

You can do a free 30 second assessment of your love language style at fivelovelanguages.com. Have your lover do it, too! By reading up on this stuff, you'll know how to show them affection in a way that they really value, which will definitely help keep you both happy!

Having said this, some relationships have problems which go deep, or which have been a part of their existence for such a long time that it seems almost impossible to dig it up and root it out. In this kind of scenario, it can be immensely useful to get some couples counselling. A counsellor can help provide a non-judgmental space to express yourselves, as well as giving you homework assignments and suggesting new ways to approach problems. While you might love to vent to your best friend, she is always going to be on your side and is not actually as objective as you think she is! Sometimes, an impartial outsider can be worth their weight in gold.

Within the U.S.A., you can find a comprehensive list of registered relationship counsellors at family-marriage-counseling.com. If you're outside America, some smart Googling should set you right!

* * *

STALE RELATIONSHIPS

What if you're in a relationship which isn't lighting your fire any more? It is my belief that even though relationships require work, they should never feel like a hardship or torture of any kind! You have free will and don't have to do anything you don't want to do. Sex should never feel like a chore. You should enjoy spending time together, making plans for the future, and loving, supporting, and encouraging each other through, well, pretty much everything.

A lot of people stay in relationships because it's convenient, safe and comfortable, but the love has dissipated. You still love one another, but you're not IN love any more. You feel like siblings: close, loving, connected, but not passionate. You know what? That happens sometimes. It doesn't make you a bad person. But when you realise that this has happened, it's important to take action. Often, we're in denial about the whole thing, and then one day it strikes us like a bolt of lightning. No one wants to wake up, screaming, "Oh my god! I'm not in love with you any more, I just love you, and I want more than this!"

This realisation might make you feel bad. What if your partner is still in love with you? The whole situation can be boiled down to a Facebook status: it's complicated. But let's face facts. Staying in a relationship out of obligation is awful. How would you feel if your partner was only with you because they felt obligated to be there?

Surely, you'd feel TERRIBLE. You'd say, "Oh for God's sake, go free, make yourself happy!" Right? Break-ups can be awful and painful, but they can open the doors for so much positivity. Here's another slightly contentious opinion: while a divorce is hard on a family, I think children learn more positive things from parents who go their separate ways, respect one another and pursue happiness, than parents who fight all the time and hate one another. What does staying in a bad relationship teach your kids?

I'm simply not convinced that we're supposed to be with one person for the rest of our lives. I think we meet people who are right for us during each stage of our personal journey, we stay with them for as long as our paths coincide, and then when that time is done, the relationship will naturally wind down. It is very rare to meet someone who is growing, progressing, and changing at exactly the same rate as you, and I don't think it is fair for anyone to expect their partner to alter their life when it is not what is best for both of you.

Sure, it can be really hard to leave a relationship where nothing is really "wrong" except that the thrill is gone. You might be plagued by doubts, thinking that if you end this relationship with what's-his-face, you'll be shipped off to Sad Gal Island. Honestly, it will not be like that. I'm not saying it will be easy, because break-ups can totally suck, but you will get through it. I promise!

It's moments like these where it can be really valuable to keep a journal, because you can flick back through the years and be reminded that you had a life (and a wonderful one at that!) before you met your current partner... and that it will continue to be wonderful even if you leave.

If you're in the midst of a real should-I-stay-or-should-I-go-now dilemma, listen to your intuition. You ALWAYS know the right thing to do, you just need to make space and time to listen to your inner self. If that fails, think about what you would tell your best friend if she was in your position, then act on it.

* * *

WHEN LOVE IS DONE

Break-ups are rough. Whether you instigated it or not, it can be a painful and heart-wrenching thing to go through, especially when you've been together for a long time and have come to rely on your partner being around. Often, our lover becomes our best friend, and the idea of losing a boy- or girlfriend as well as a best friend in one fell swoop is almost too much to deal with.

The good news is that your friends are still there for you, and while they may not be able to provide the same level of intimate support as your partner once did, they will be able to do a pretty swell job. If you abandoned your friends in the early days of love and lust, don't blame yourself -- we're all guilty of that at some point. Sure, now that your relationship is over, you might feel a bit pathetic crawling back to your buddies, but if they are true friends, they'll be able to forgive you. Then you can get down to the much-needed business of going out together all the time, dissecting every facet of your now ex-relationship, and scouting for eligible bachelor/ettes!

My number one break-up tip is as follows: save yourself a trip to the institution by staying away from your ex for as long as you can. Impose a ban on contact, and stick to it. Tell your friends that you're doing this, and have them hold you accountable. My rule is typically six months of radio silence. I say to my now ex-lover, "I am not going to talk to you for six months, and if you try to contact me I am going to pretend you don't exist, because we need time to get over this and move on". They often get huffy, and tell me I am being ridiculous, but after a while they realise I'm right! Look, buddy, I have been through enough break-ups to know the protocol!

Whenever someone goes through a break-up and comes to me for advice, I tell them to stay away from their ex, and they say, "Oh but we're such good friends, we don't need that", blah blah blah. Then after a month and a half of total, non-stop BULLSHIT, they come to me and concede my point, while I try my very best not to say "I told you so".

The reasons for staying away from your ex are trillionfold. Staying friends with your ex-lover is rife with ulterior motive. One of you got dumped, so that person will probably be hurting and at some point, they might decide you're the best target to take that hurt out on. If one of you gets involved with someone else, the other person is going to feel... well, let's just say "crazy" and leave it at that. You no longer have each other's best interests at heart, and will behave badly. Very badly.

Break-ups can be a real eye-opener, because when they happen, you learn what your ex is really like. Someone who used to be supportive and chill becomes a psycho hose-beast, sending emails full of back-handed compliments and complaining about stuff that really doesn't matter any more. And here's some food for thought: do you really want to be the person your ex comes to when their new lover isn't doing x or y and they want sympathy? No. No you do not. You are not going to have sympathy for them in that situation. You are more likely to want to beat them senseless with a huge mallet!

You'll never be able to move on from them if they are still in your life all the time. You need to be able to forget they ever existed, at least for a little while, and deal with the emotions you're feeling without them hanging out in your living room every weekend. So, believe me, save yourself the drama, and break contact. Be an adult, suck it up, move on. You do not need them around you, you survived before them, you will survive after them. Trust me. (Also, in a few months, you'll think, 'Wow, I sure am glad they're gone!', and it's a great feeling.)

By the way, when I say, "Stay away from your ex", I mean this in all senses of the word. You may refrain from calling them at midnight, but if you can't stop refreshing their Instagram feed, you are being weird and stalky. This will not aid you in moving on. It will just suck you deeper into the maelstrom. Remove them from your Facebook news feed (or just remove them as a friend entirely), take them off your Twitter list, and stop reading their stupid blog, in ADDITION to deleting their phone number, archiving all their old emails, and putting away all the stuff which makes you think about them. Don't worry about how their feelings might be hurt if you take them off any of your social networking sites -- it's really not the time to be sensitive and sympathetic. Get a bit Nike on it, and Just Do It. You'll feel better.

It's really helpful to institute a grieving period, in which you give yourself permission to behave as shockingly as you dare. Cry all the time, drink yourself into a stupor if you must, talk about your ex until your tongue goes raw around the edges, whatever you like, but you have to put a deadline on it. Flip through your calendar, choose a date (a month, two months, six months from now) and on that day, write, "GET OVER IT". Hopefully by the time you get to that page, you will be so well past that that it will take a moment for you to remember what it's all about, but the point is that it's wonderful to be able to wallow. If you really allow yourself to get deep into the hideousness, odds are excellent that you'll get so fed up with yourself that you'll move on much more quickly.

Other things to keep in mind:

♥ Spend plenty of time with your friends. You will need them to keep you on the straight and narrow, as well as to provide you with much-needed entertainment and distraction. Be good to them. You might want to spare their ears from time to time, so write at least a portion of your relationship-related madness in your journal, as opposed to leaving them long, rambling voicemails every morning at 4am.

♥ Be good to yourself as well. This is a great time to commit to a new exercise regime or start eating healthily. Cut out drinking wine, or eating cheese, or start doing yoga in the morning. It will give you something else to think about, and make you feel good at the same time.

♥ Don't try and seek revenge, no matter how evil your ex was to you. Remember, all the energy you invest in them is time you could be spending making yourself happy! Living well is the best revenge!

♥ Find some kind of outlet, or at least something to do. Take a creative writing class or burlesque lessons. It will give you a sense of satisfaction, and will also keep you away from the telephone, because sometimes you will find yourself sitting next to it with very itchy fingers. And on that note...

♥ Don't get back together with them without a lot of consideration.

I know it's tempting, but hold off. More importantly, please, for the love of all that is holy, don't sleep with them again! If you get back together immediately, odds are excellent that the reasons you broke up with them in the first place are still there. When it comes to sex, you are simply entering a world of pain. While one of you might have the presence of mind to know that it is "just sex", there is a huge emotional attachment still lingering, which will confuse at least one, if not both of you. The best hanky-panky in the world isn't worth the emotional turmoil that you'll end up dealing with. Like I said above, just cut them off. Removing them as an option from your life is the easiest way to do things.

♥ Think about yourself for a change! It's so easy to get swept away in your partner's plans -- or the plans you've made together -- that you forget about yourself, who you are and what you want. You don't listen to your favourite band because your girlfriend hates them, you stop running because chilling on the couch with your boyfriend sounds much more appealing, and the list goes on. Take time to rediscover who you are! It's FUN, and definitely time well spent.

The real thing to remember is that even though being in love and exploring relationships can be painful at times, it's part of what makes us human. Without these strange personal interactions, our lives would be so much less interesting. Wherever your love journey takes you, and no matter how wild or tame it may be, you will still always learn valuable lessons, grow in previously unimagined ways, and keep evolving, hopefully for the better. It would be magnificent to be able to say that all relationships go well, but unfortunately, this is not the case. However, I still think that even in a horrible relationship, there are things to be learned and opportunities for positive change buried within. Often these awful situations make us stronger, better people. It's really all about attitude.

Whatever happens to you in the name of love, I hope that you can use your experiences to catapult you into a future which is brighter and more fabulous than you could have ever imagined. Remember to keep taking risks, and stay open-hearted!

To put it simply, you gotta be in love with your wonderful self. You should be able to look in the mirror, pout, flick your hair, wink at yourself and think, "Babe, you are divine."

#RSLBOOK

HOMEWORK

♥ CONSIDER YOUR OLD PATTERNS.

Is there a certain type of person you always go for? Are you attracted to the bad boy or the good girl? Do you tend to get involved with people who treat you with a lack of respect? It's time to dive deep, and think about why you keep repeating these patterns.

♥ MAKE A LIST OF ATTRIBUTES THAT YOU'RE LOOKING FOR.

Remember not to be too superficial! Ruminate on this for a while: there's no rush. Think about what would enhance your life. If, after reviewing your old patterns, you know that there are things you don't want in your love match, simply write the opposite of that trait on your list. So, if your ex was surrounded by chaos, maybe you'd write peaceful. Or organised. Always keep it positive!

♥ PRACTICE HAVING REAL, OPEN CONVERSATIONS.

You may not be in a relationship right now, and that's okay. You can get plenty of practice in learning to effectively communicate your wants and needs with your friends, workmates, and family. Become comfortable with asking for what you want, and don't be dissuaded if it takes a while, most of us are out of practice! Next time you have a disagreement with your friend, open up a dialogue about it, rather than pretending it never happened. All of this stuff will stand you in good stead when true love comes knockin'.

♥ DROP YOUR RELIANCE ON SARCASM AND PLAY-FIGHTING.

It only leads to bickering and festering resentment. Instead, make a pact to only say what you mean with your friends, family, and lovers.

♥ KEEP PUTTING YOURSELF OUT THERE, AND CONTINUE ENJOYING YOUR LIFE!

You may not meet the babe of your dreams tomorrow, but if your life is full of fun and positive friendships, it won't matter so much. The best relationships always happen when your life is already great. No one wants to date someone who has nothing going on, so explore the things that make you tick, and resolve to enjoy life, no matter whether you have a lover or not!

BEST FRIENDS FOREVER

Keeping your friendships fresh,
finding platonic soulmates, and clearing
out the fakes, phonies and meanies!

L oneliness is not just for people who live in cabins like hermits, or who never leave their houses. A lot of us are lonely and hardly even realise it, because loneliness can manifest in many different ways. If you often find yourself feeling excluded or like no one really understands, or if you find it hard to talk to people about what you're feeling, it could just be that you're lonely.

Sadly, loneliness is part of the modern human condition. We spend so much time in front of our computers and staring into our phones, and while we might be "talking" to our friends or peers all day, we're lacking the deep, connected, face-to-face personal interactions that used to be an essential part of life.

One of the hardest things to stomach is the feeling of loneliness while you're in a committed relationship. We've all bought into the fantasy that our perfect partner will tick all our boxes, as well as being a riveting conversationalist, a great listener, and sharing many of our interests. This is so rarely the case! It is, quite frankly, mad to expect one person to be able to provide us with everything we need from the outside world. That is why most of us have a variety of people we spend time with, or go to for advice. Our friends all bring something different to the table.

I have some friends I talk to about business, some who love to riff on spirituality, a bunch who consider themselves sexperts, and a special few I can talk to about absolutely anything. That's the great thing about friends: they bring diversity, breadth and width to your life.

The good news is that if you feel lonely, ironically, you are not alone. A lot of people feel that way and it's totally okay. They don't all go off the deep end! Even better than that, with just a simple switch in your thinking (or belief systems), you'll realise that the world is full of people who can supply you with those things you crave. Want someone you can talk with frankly about your sexuality? Desperate for some political debate? Hankering for a feminine role model or mentor? Even if you just want someone you can go and get a manicure with, or someone you can send frantic text messages to about whether your outfit works or not, there is someone out there who will fill that gap, someone who can be that person for you. You just have to find them!

The idea of "making friends" can make us all feel a bit coy, a bit juvenile. I mean, how are you supposed to make friends as a bonafide adult?! Awkward!

Except it's not awkward at all, or at least, it doesn't have to be. It's as easy as putting on a smile, and approaching someone with a friendly tone. I've met plenty of people that way, although I have to say that I met the majority of my long-lasting, deep, and true BFFs online first.

I know this might sound a little hypocritical, given that just a few seconds ago, I talked about how constant use of the internet makes us all feel more separate and lonely. This is true, but the benefit of the internet is that it's easy for the people who really get you to find you.

Before I discovered the internet in 1996, the only people I really knew were girls from school. I went to a private Anglican girls' school, and let's just say that I didn't exactly fit in. I'd be reading American Psycho in the back row while my peers were talking about their next waterpolo tournament. Compound this with the fact that I was a diehard goth trapped in an itchy green uniform, and imagine my anguish!

As soon as our home was wired up with a 33.6kbps modem, my experience of the world changed. I had a lifeline, and was instantly connected to people who had the same interests as I did. I was able to research the things I loved, and learn so much. It was like being given the keys to the kingdom; I felt like I was free.

My interest in the internet quickly turned into a full-blown obsession. There was so much to read, to learn, to discover... How could an episode of some sitcom even begin to compete?

If I wasn't at school, I was online, finding people to talk to. Pretty quickly, those online friendships started to bleed over into real life. I stumbled across a group of teenagers and people in their early twenties who lived in my city and loved everything I did. I went to meet one of them -- outside a Subway sandwich shop, naturally -- and was invited into their circle of friends.

These people were fascinating to me, but they were also interested in me and taught me new things. They became my new role models and advice givers. It meant a lot to me to have friends who were older, with whom I could have intelligent conversations, and it made me feel good about myself. I started to feel a little less alien, and a little more accepting of my own weirdness. I drifted away from my friends at school, and spent my weekends with this other group, instead.

Those people really set the benchmark for what I would expect from social interactions in later years. For example, I wanted to talk with my friends, rather than drink to oblivion all night. I wanted my social group to be a motley crew of unusual people, from wildly different backgrounds and with a penchant for rebellion. That's definitely a theme that has been consistent in my life!

Meeting those people, both online and off, taught me that there were no limits. We didn't need to be alike in age or location to connect, and it made me realise that friendships of convenience were not the only option. My friends were people I sought out, and that hasn't changed. In fact, as time goes on, I am even less hesitant about making friends with people who live in London, Minneapolis, or Tokyo, because now I can travel wherever I like!

I've come to realise that people who use the internet like I do -- in a kind of compulsive, obsessive manner -- are the sort of people I like. People who are online as much as me are curious, creative, socially-conscious and dialed in. If you're an internet fiend like I am, don't look past the web as an incredible source of possible friendships.

FEMALE FRIENDSHIPS

When I was younger, I was guilty of putting my boyfriends first. In fact, I didn't have a lot of female friends, but that is probably no big surprise. Since I was always best friends with my boyfriend, his group of friends became my group of friends. The only women I really knew were dating his male friends. I didn't seek out female companionship, and I was okay with that.

But when I moved to New York City in 2008, that all changed. I didn't have a boyfriend to rely on, and I started to meet people under my own steam. I began to discover all of these amazing women who had their own businesses and blogs, were doing their own thing, and kicking major amounts of ass. It was really inspiring to meet women like this in the flesh, and as time goes by, I value having these women in my life even more.

I prioritise spending time with my girlfriends: it is essential. It's like having a genius girl coven, who get you, who love to laugh with you, and can give you advice and lift you up when you need it.

A lot of women don't have many female friends, and that's okay, but if this is resonating with you, I'd encourage you to seek out more babes to spend time with. We're constantly being taught to see women as competition, rather than people who need you and can make your life better. Make the mental leap, and fuck the status quo! We are so much more powerful when we're together!

* * *

MAKING FRIENDS

Don't be intimidated by the name of this segment. Keep in mind that you are already surrounded by people who know you, and so you don't need to go out and meet a new slew of weirdos in order to form great friendships or have a banging social life. In fact, if you made a list of all the people you already know -- relatives, workmates, friends of the family, people you once worked with, members of groups or religious organisations you're a part of, people you went to school with, their families, etc., you'd be quite shocked at the vastness of your social network.

Don't judge a book by its cover too much! If you ask the right questions, you'll discover that anyone can be fascinating! If ever you want to tap into that pool of people, it's as easy as making a phone-call or sending an email. The situation is never as dire as you think!

I have met people in the most unlikely places. Once I responded to the Craigslist advertisement of a man from the U.S.A. who was in Auckland for a few weeks and wanted an activity companion. Friendships have blossomed in Las Vegas over buffet dinners, I've had fascinating conversations with people on airplanes, and I've met girls online who later cuddled me through heartbreak. In a lot of ways, you get out of friendship what you put into it: you have to make the effort, and put yourself out there.

Realistically, making a friend is as easy as starting a conversation... But here are some things that will make your quest a little easier!

Practice smiling

I know this sounds a little bizarre, but seriously: do it! Practice smiling at people when you pass them in the street, when they get into the elevator with you, when you order your food. You will find, overwhelmingly, that most people will respond in kind. (Those who don't are probably just having a bad day, so don't take it personally!) Smiling makes you feel good, and is like getting your training wheels in being social. It's a way of breaking you out of your comfort zone, which needs to happen if you want to start meeting new people!

Practice saying hello

This is like adding an extra step into your smile practice, and now, you're involving your vocal cords! Again, you'll discover that most people will say hello back, and some will even enter into conversation with you.

Give compliments

Everyone loves a good, sincere compliment! It's a fun thing to work on, too, because it trains you to look for the positive in people, even those with whom you might think you have nothing in common. Start with the little things, like telling someone that their skirt or shoes are cool, and move on to giving compliments about personality or intelligence. The old saying of "Flattery will get you everywhere" is more true than you can imagine.

Take off your headphones!

As much as I understand the glory of walking around the city with your own personal soundtrack, try to look at it from the point of view of a potential friend. If you go to the supermarket, gym, or library with your headphones on, no one is going to attempt to talk to you because you look unapproachable! You look like you're in your own little world and you don't need anyone else. Now, maybe none of these things are true; maybe you just can't get enough of the swelling symphonies being piped directly into your brain. Trust me, I get it! I am a music obsessive, too. The problem is that people who see you on the street don't know these things. There is no context. They might think you look interesting, but because you have headphones on, they don't want to be a bother. And so it goes!

Avoid bars

They're just not the best places to meet people. I mean, if you're looking for a casual fling, it's probably a good place to look, but if you're trying to unearth a potential new best friend, you'll find it more difficult. The only thing people in a bar have in common is that they want to get their drink on, and unless that is your #1 interest, there are much better places to find people with obsessions like yours. The likelihood that you will have something in common with the person you're standing next to at the bar is low. Don't sweat it if you haven't had much luck in bars, pubs or clubs. It's not really the most fertile ground for anything valuable.

Place an ad!

This sounds a little odd, I admit, but I speak from experience when I say that it's really fun and worth trying. Years ago, I had broken up with my boyfriend, and was low on friends. I decided to submit an ad in a local paper which had a "Looking For Friends" column.

I can't remember the specific details, but I'm pretty sure it described me as a "22 year old enfant terrible and picnic enthusiast", and that my favourite book was Lolita. (You can only imagine the kind of people who came out of the woodwork, right?!) I ended up with a lot of interesting responses on my answering machine!

These days, you could easily use an online service for something like this, although to me, there's nothing like seeing it in print. It's fun to see who responds, and it's an excellent way to meet people outside of your normal social circle.

Remember that most people are really pretty simple

Everybody wants to be liked. Even if the person you're speaking to is spouting off all kinds of rubbish, see if you can find a grain of truth in what they're saying and go along with it. This makes for a much more pleasant conversation, not to mention it is good practice in trying to see another person's point of view. Always remember that people want to feel loved and accepted, and they want to be made to feel special, too. If you can really focus on them -- eye contact and being really present in the moment help a lot here -- they will think very highly of you. Check A Guide To Manners For The Modern Minx (Chapter 8) for more tips on social graces!

The world is full of people, and all of them have something wonderful to offer, even if you can't see it immediately. It's worth making the effort, and trying to get to know strangers. You never know where it could lead! We should all be honoured that people want to spend time with us and get to know us. As long as the people in your life make you feel good about yourself, you're on the right track.

* * *

ON KEEPING FRIENDS

If 80 percent of success is, as Woody Allen once said, just showing up, then 80 percent of building and maintaining relationships is just staying in touch.

Friendships require upkeep. Unfortunately, you can't just hang out with someone a couple of times and expect to remain friendly. It just doesn't work that way. People are busy, and we are all constantly meeting new people, so if you don't make an effort to stay on someone's radar, they will start to forget about you. This can be frustrating, but there are ways around it!

I have a friend who sits down every Sunday to connect with his friends. He typically does it by email, since it's easiest that way, and it's something he learned from the book Never Eat Alone by Keith Ferrazzi. In the book, Keith Ferrazzi describes this practice of connecting regularly with people as "pinging".

The whole idea behind "pinging" is that if you're going to go to all the trouble of meeting people, you should follow up! We all meet so many people that very few stick in our minds unless they do something to differentiate themselves. While "pinging" is mostly something that you do to business contacts, it makes sense to extend the practice to your friends and acquaintances too. While you don't want to be a pest in an otherwise clogged inbox, sending an email every month or two certainly isn't intrusive, and will most likely be extremely welcome.

It would be amazing if everyone did this, but the fact is that people don't, so sometimes you'll find that you need to be the person who keeps things moving. You need to make the phone-call, or organise lunch, or call up just to say hello. Think of fun activities and invite your friends. My friends are an infinitely busy bunch, but it's not hard to stay in touch. We send emails back and forth, ask advice, plan activities and vacations, and plot evil schemes! You don't need to send an essay; something as simple as, "I saw this dress and thought you might like it!" with a link is a sweet way to show your friends you're thinking of them, and can easily lead to a bigger conversation. Remember, it should be fun to reach out to your friends! If it isn't, why do you have them?!

A note: if, despite your best efforts, your friendship feels really one-sided, say something about that to your friend. Sometimes people are just forgetful, and need to be reminded to make time for their friends! However, if they don't seem to care, then at least you'll know, and you can both move on. This may be painful, but it's always good to know the truth. Plus, once you clear them out of your life, there will be a lot more room for rad people to step in and take their place!

It's vital to make time for your friends. Modern life is so frantic that we feel like we barely have time to breathe, let alone to hang out with our friends and have fun. The reality is that if your friendships are important to you, you will find the time for them, and -- crucially -- if you don't make the time, your friends will simply forget about you. Harsh but true! We would all like to think that we are so wonderful and memorable that our friends will forgive us anything, but that is seldom the case. Your friend has feelings, and if you reject them often enough, they will naturally gravitate to someone else. It's the same with any kind of relationship: that initial spark starts to fade, and if you want to keep things feeling fresh and magical, you have to work at it.

✳ ✳ ✳

WHAT SHOULD WE DO TOGETHER?

Why, anything you like!

Humans like routine and repetition, which is why most of us go to the same old restaurants all the time, and order the exact same meal. The same goes for the activities we engage in with our friends. After a while, though, things start to feel stale. I mean, how many times can you go to a bar with the same people before it begins to bore you to tears?

I have a very low boredom threshold, which means I have to be creative and -- most importantly -- proactive. I can't sit around and wait for someone to suggest something wild, because it will probably never happen. I have to start dreaming up weird things myself, and then follow through! Once you start doing this, it gets kind of addictive, and best of all, it brings a massive amount of adventure and excitement to your life.

Try suggesting some of these ideas to your friends. Then go and do them!

Plan a party. Take an art class. Stalk and obsess over cute people. Have a date and make vision or mood or inspiration boards (all you need are corkboards, pins, old magazines and coffee!). Go on a picnic. Visit the botanic gardens. Bake cakes for one another. Have a marathon of your favourite show. Go urban exploring with your cameras. Dress up super-fancy and go to the supermarket. Play tennis and pretend to be aristocrats. Go on a boat trip. Devote time to attending one bizarre sounding art show a week. Hold up "Free Hugs" signs in public places. Decide to throw a monthly event together! Plan a road trip to a strange monument. Travel. Take a cruise. Teach one another how to make your favourite dishes. Have dinner parties for all your friends every couple of weeks! Drink cocktails in the sunshine. Have a miniature celebration with bacon sandwiches. Volunteer together. Swap clothes. Start a book club. Write letters to one another! Go to an amusement park. Take photobooth pictures. Make a YouTube channel. Start a blog about your adventures. Make sandcastles. Go miniature golfing. Email your friends and ask if you can help them out with anything. Learn to make absinthe! Participate in parades and festivals. Audition for plays. Take dance classes. Have a slumber party! Look through old photos and laugh your heads off. Read old sections of your journals aloud. Go to a museum and just hang out in your favourite room. Be tourists in your own city. Go shopping. Get pedicures. Bake cookies in funny shapes; write obscene things on them; give them out. Climb trees. Sneak onto a rooftop. Dance all day. Hug it out. Abduct one of your friends for a miscellaneous adventure. Give out flowers to strangers. Play hopscotch. Draw on the sidewalk with chalk. Glamourbomb! Blow bubbles in crowds. Tuck secret messages into library books. Start a fun project together and get stickers made. Read each others' palms. Wear ridiculous hats. Eat candy all day. Ride carousels. Do yoga. Make jewellery together. Dye your hair. Get tattoos. Eat watermelon...

You get the idea!

FUSSIN' AND FIGHTIN'

Fighting with your friends is awful. There's nothing like that sinking feeling in your stomach when you realise that things have turned sour, and there's no easy way to salvage them. It's not a sensation I would wish on anyone.

We all have different ways of dealing with conflict. Some people like to avoid it, and others rush straight in to try to clear things up. It all depends on how you're wired. The way that you deal with conflict will dictate how your friendship evolves. Let's say you're annoyed at your friend for saying something insensitive. if you never mention it to her, she will probably continue in that same insensitive vein, until one day you explode with rage! That is not a recipe for a happy friendship.

My friend Gabby Bernstein says, "Don't be afraid of conflict. Instead, see it as an opportunity to gain clarity." When we reframe disagreements this way, we can see them as a window to enlightenment, and even a way to move to closer to our friend in the future.

I am keen on peace-making, and even if I think the other person is 100% wrong, I will often be the first person to extend the olive branch. Disagreements and bad blood make me so uncomfortable that I'd rather it was just over so we can move the hell on. Now, this is not to say that I enjoy having to be the peacemaker all the time, but the relief of having something sorted out is, to me, totally worth it.

Ask yourself: is it more important to be "right", or to preserve the friendship? For me, maintaining the friendship is always more valuable, and I don't see the point in letting your pride (or need to be right) get in the way. Clutching onto resentment is so bad for you, emotionally, physically, and spiritually. I would rather open up the conversation and wade through the muck to a resolution than shut down, dwell, and become incandescently furious every time I think about it!

Life is simply too short to hold grudges. What's the point? Holding a grudge is like drinking poison and waiting for the other person to die. Buddy Hackett said, "I've had a few arguments with people, but I never carry a grudge. You know why? While you're carrying a grudge, they're out dancing." Bingo! Most of the time, the person you're mad at doesn't even know it! They are going about their life, blissfully unaware, while you're seething somewhere. Clutching onto your anger -- which is all about your ego -- is a massive waste of time and energy. Why, you could be baking a cake, instead!

If your friend has done something truly unforgivable, then I would encourage you to cut them out of your life, but if it's just a simple disagreement or miscommunication, try to leave your ego out of it as much as possible. There is no "right" or "wrong", only two people in a mess.

When someone hurts your feelings, it might take time before you want to see or talk to them again, but there's no point in prolonging the rage. When you feel that you're ready, get back in touch. Say you're sorry, and that you value their friendship more than you care about some stupid disagreement. Send them love, and be sincere. Hopefully, all will be right in the end.

✳ ✳ ✳

FRIENDSHIP KILLERS

Jealousy and competition

Why? Because there's nothing worse than a friend who doesn't have your real interests at heart, or is suspicious of you, or secretly wishes you weren't as great as you are.

How to fix it: Learn to appreciate how great you are. Practice more radical self love! Recognise that comparing yourself to anyone is always a losing game, and that the answer is that you have to get comfortable in your own skin. Sometimes, too, it helps to just be honest about it. Sit down with your friend and tell them how you feel! Honesty is always the best policy.

Being constantly late

Why? Because it shows that you don't value your friend's time.

How to fix it: Simply make the decision that you're not going to be late anymore. When I first got to Manhattan, I would drastically miscalculate travelling times, and I was late more times than I could count. The next year, one of my resolutions was to be early to my appointments. Plan accordingly, and leave earlier! Anyone can do this, you just need to make the decision to do it.

Cancelling get-togethers

Why? Because, again, it shows that you don't value your friend's time... And it makes them think you didn't want to see them in the first place!

How to fix it: Stop committing to dates that you can't keep! We all work long days and sometimes by the time 8pm rolls around, leaving the house again is the last thing we want to do. If going out at night simply does not float your boat, make lunch dates instead. Work out when you're most likely to want to see your friends, and schedule accordingly!

Not returning phone-calls, texts, or emails

Why? Because it makes your friend feel unimportant and like you don't care about them.

How to fix it: This one is easy: just do it! Make a note to call your buddy back if you always forget after you've listened to voicemail.

Dishonesty

Why? Self-explanatory, surely!

How to fix it: Start telling the truth. Some people tell little "white lies" all the time, because that's how they were raised, but that doesn't make it okay. Just be honest. If you find that difficult, you might want to look at what's causing you to lie. Are you afraid to tell the truth, or is there something else going on? Some self-reflection will serve you well here. If what you discover disturbs or worries you, you might want to talk to a therapist about it -- they are experts, after all!

Complaining or negativity

Why? Because it pulls down the energy of everyone around you, and cements you as a psychic vampire!

How to fix it: If you've noticed people tell you that you complain a lot, take it as an opportunity for growth and positive change. A lot of us whine and moan without even realising it. To top it all off, a lot of us learn, subconsciously, that complaining helps us bond with other people. Start listening to yourself when you talk. Take notice of what you're really saying. Speaking more positively is just like changing any kind of habit: once you become aware of it, come up with ways to alter the behaviour. Ask a friend to keep you in check, or journal your progress. This is really something worth working on, I promise!

SEVERING A FRIENDSHIP

Sometimes, after a bit of reflection, we come to the terrible realisation that we don't really like our friends anymore. Don't beat yourself up if this describes your current situation. It's very easy to end up with a lot of negative friends, or simply friends who bore us, especially in your teens or early twenties. We're all so insecure and unsure at that time that we often accept anyone who wants in. The kicker is that misery loves company, and negative or sad people want nothing more than to pull you down to their level. If you have ambitions and actually want to make something of your life, having the sad patrol around you is only going to make it more difficult. You don't need that!

Our influences shape us into the person we are. If your friends have eating disorders, it is likely your eating will become disordered also. If your boyfriend gets angry in traffic, you will probably find yourself road-raging along with him. If your best friend hates men, before long, you will start to agree with her!

This happens because of evolution. Just like monkeys, humans have what are called mirror neurons, and this is how, as a species, we learn: by watching and imitating those around us. Mirror neurons are an essential part of our evolutionary survival, and because of this, they tick over, below the surface, at all times.

So even though you may have no intention of becoming like the people around you, if your mother is miserable, your girlfriend is homicidal, and your best friend is a misogynist, you will unconsciously begin to mimic and imitate all these behaviours. Unless you want to be just like them, the best thing you can do is extricate yourself from these people.

I feel that I can speak to this subject with some authority, because I used to be part of the misery brigade. My friends and I hated our lives, and everything we experienced was proof that the world was shit. We were engaged in a vicious feedback loop. At the time, I thought that being sad, not eating, and having constant drama in my life made me more "interesting". I thought that happy people were stupid and annoying (really, this was just misguided jealousy!). My friends and I didn't want to be "normal", we wanted to be different goddamnit, and we were willing to suffer to be that way.

Thankfully, once I stepped away from that group of people, I learned the error of my ways. Being happy doesn't make you normal at all -- in fact, happy people are in the minority. It is easy to throw your hands up in frustration, and be tragic and defeatist. It is also incredibly boring. Truth time: people don't enjoy being around negative whiners. It's mind-numbingly dull, which is the ultimate crime!

Let's say your friend's primary interest is being judgmental, and you end up being like that, too. A typical exchange between the two of you might go something like this:

Your friend: "Ugh, look at that girl! She is so disgusting. I would never leave the house if I looked like that!"

You: "I know, right?! We are so much cuter!"

Remember that we can never change the way other people behave, we can only ever change the way we react to them. Basically, if you stop encouraging their bad behaviour, they will eventually stop being so revolting. So, instead of responding in kind, you could change the subject, or you could just tell them that making remarks about other people is boring and mean, and that you're striving to be more positive. They will soon learn that they can't have those conversations with you, and so they will either change their tune, or drift to other people who want to share in the hatred. It's like having a child who throws tantrums — if you ignore it, they will stop, or try it elsewhere.

It also helps to establish strong boundaries. If you want to remain friends, remember that they're not going to change unless they want to. When they start being negative, let them know that you're no longer interested in listening. Maybe they'll respect you for saying this, and maybe not. If they do, then that's wonderful! Score a point for you! If not, as above, they will move away from you. It's a win-win situation.

We teach people how to treat us, so don't be shy or coy about letting your friends know when their behaviour is unacceptable.

The other option is to cut contact entirely, which is probably only best in really extreme circumstances. Don't read their emails, delete their telephone number, remove them from your social networks, and stop reading their blog. Cold turkey, baby! Sometimes, it's the only way to break free.

✳ ✳ ✳

NEXT LEVEL BFFS

Most friendships will deepen naturally over time. Going away on holiday, starting a business together, or being there for major life events will speed up the process, but sometimes you'll notice that you've had a friend for a couple of years, and it never seems to get any deeper.

The reason for that is because you haven't shown one another your vulnerability. If you don't share what's really going on in your lives, your friendship will never intensify or grow, and will continue floating along the surface. Sometimes that's perfect: you don't need to be sharing your deepest, darkest secrets with everyone you meet. But if you want to get closer to your friend, you have to open up. You have to soften and let them in. It can't be all bravado and rowdy drinking games and talk of conquests. You have to discuss your insecurities, worries, hopes, dreams, and fears.

It's also vital to be honest. If you can't tell your friends the truth, what's the point? We don't need sycophants in our lives, or people who will unnecessarily inflate our egos while withholding what they might really think about us. I'd rather have an honest enemy than a double-dealing pseudo-chum!

Telling the truth can be hard. Years ago, one of my friends -- totally out of the blue -- told me she was engaged, and was going to get married a week later. I was delighted for her, but I was also nervous: she had only known this guy a couple of months, and had recently gone through a grisly break-up.

I was unsure how to respond. As a friend, I think the most valuable thing we can give one another is our honesty; I am not the girl who'll say, "You should buy that dress!" when it is too tight across your hips. So I started composing a response.

My boyfriend said, "You should just tell her she's crazy!", and that's exactly what he would have done, if his friend had told him something similar. But that is not my style! I wanted to tell her how I felt, so I could go to sleep that night without a guilty conscience, knowing I had done the right thing. But I didn't want to offend her. My response was written from my point of view and my own thoughts on marriage; thoughts on my own relationship, not hers. After all, who am I to tell her about her relationship?

I said that I was really excited for her, and that I totally understood her excitement. I also told her that even though I wanted to marry my boyfriend, I realised that there was no rush. Neither of us were going anywhere. I wrote about how important it was to have a strong foundation of friendship, because it is the only thing which lasts, and that there are so many serious things you both need to consider before you commit to being with someone for the rest of your life. I said that I loved her, and would support her whatever she did, but that divorce is a bitch, and it would be really smart of her to get to know this guy before they eloped. I didn't want to rain on her parade or be a dreamkiller, but that there was no rush or urgency.

I was anxious as I waited for her response. I knew she might be offended: after all, she hadn't asked for my opinion. I thought she might tell me to mind my own business. Thankfully, that's not how it played out. She appreciated my honesty, and said that she had gotten swept away. She wasn't offended by my advice, and she was grateful for people who were willing to step up and speak their truth.

Of course, she ended up marrying the guy, and they are still together today... So what do I know?!

That's one reason our friendship has lasted and why it is so strong. We are honest with one another, and we don't pull any punches. We also respect one another's opinion, which goes a long way! Real friendships are about honesty, tact, respect, and eventually, having things in common. Lots of people grow apart because their idea of what constitutes a fun time changes, but if you have all the aforementioned things and both think doing x or y together is your idea of the best night ever, then your friendship has an unshakeable foundation.

* * *

CAN WE REALLY BE FRIENDS FOR LIFE?

There are three types of friends in our lives: friends for a season, friends for a reason and friends for life. Friends for a season are people who are great company for a short time, when circumstances are right, but as our lives change, the friendship drifts apart. Friends for a reason are those who have something to teach us, something to learn from us, or are just friends of convenience, like when you work or live together. Friends for life are the most rare group, and of course, these friendships are the most important to maintain. They are the people who really are with us through thick and thin, no matter how great or terrible our lives are. They always have time for us, they have our back, and they love us beyond measure.

When you find a friend who has those qualities, you have stumbled upon a rare gem. Maintain that friendship as best you can. Friendships like this aren't just ways to pass the time or people to talk to at parties, they are support systems: an integral part of life, and a major source of happiness. Having someone you can rely on no matter what is the most incredible, blissful feeling, and absolutely worth pursuing.

We're constantly being taught to see women as competition, rather than people who need you and can make your life better. Make the mental leap, and fuck the status quo! We are so much more powerful when we're together!

#RSLBOOK

HOMEWORK

♥ START TO "PING" YOUR FRIENDS REGULARLY.

Once you've made the effort to become friends, don't forget to stay in touch. Work "pinging" into your routine, and you'll find that your friendships naturally continue to evolve and strengthen.

♥ MAKE AN EFFORT TO SPEND MORE TIME WITH THE WOMEN YOU KNOW.

It's essential to have a coven of babes who've got your back. Do whatever you can to get together with your female friends as often as possible. It will enrich your life so much.

♥ PRACTICE GIVING SINCERE COMPLIMENTS.

It'll make you feel good, it'll make your recipient feel good, and it will fortify your social skills! Sometimes, when I walk along the street, I challenge myself to think one positive thing about everyone who walks past me. It can be tough, especially in New York City, when you pass hundreds of people in a single walk, but by the time I'm home, I'm on a high like no other!

♥ WRITE YOURSELF A CHEAT SHEET OF QUESTIONS.

If you have a secret stash of interesting questions in your mind, you'll never be lost for conversation. Come up with ten good questions, and none of that "What do you do?" stuff! If you're finding this tricky, check out Danielle LaPorte's app, called Conversation Starters. It is exactly what it sounds like, and it's brilliant!

♥ BRAINSTORM SOME FUN ACTIVITIES YOU CAN DO WITH YOUR FRIENDS.

Sit down and think about it: what would you really like to do with your favourite people? Once you've come up with a few good ideas, start to reach out and make plans! Don't blame me if you end up having the best month ever!

MANIFESTING AND MAGIC-MAKING

Using imagination and reverie
to create a perfect universe!

This is my guide to manifesting as I know and understand it. I don't know everything, but I have been studying the subject for eight years. I started to develop an interest in manifestation in early 2006, which was a hugely transformative year for me. It was the year I overcame my eating disorder, changed my name, moved to Australia, and started galadarling.com.

In 2005, I could not have possibly imagined that my life would look like this today. Back then, I believed that I was doomed to a life of misery, and I can say with absolute certainty that if I hadn't put the law of attraction into practice, there is no way I would be living this same life. I wouldn't even be writing this. I would still be in some desk job which I loathed, and living obliviously, refusing to take responsibility for my own life.

The law of attraction has a bit of a bad reputation these days, probably because some irresponsible people leapt on the bandwagon and made manifesting sound like a cosmic mail-order catalogue! I can only speak to my own experience, which is that thinking and behaving in this way has absolutely revolutionised my life. For every cynic who talks about how "it doesn't work", I can think of never-ending examples that completely contradict their point of view. That's okay, though, and I'm not interested in trying to persuade them to see it from my point of view. How other people choose to live is none of my business!

The most important thing to keep in mind when it comes to manifesting is that you have to take action. Manifesting is a two-way street: you cannot simply meditate your way to a mansion in Beverly Hills, much as you might like to!

Some people get confused about manifesting, and think it is about woo-woo thoughts and waving around a bit of sage. It isn't! Manifesting is about getting the universe to meet you halfway. It's about doing the work while having faith that things will work out for the best. It's about knowing that what you want is coming to you, but also knowing that you have to get the ball rolling. After all, if you just sit in your room thinking about what you want, but don't get out there and tell anyone about it, do any research, or take any real actionable steps, how will progress be made?

Sometimes it helps to envision manifesting as throwing a ball out to the universe and waiting for the cosmic soup to bat it back to you. It's a team effort! If the ball doesn't come back, throw out another pitch! Some of them won't come back, but many of them will. You just have to keep at it.

Learning how to manifest the best life ever isn't about sitting around, being faux-positive, and living in denial. Good things come to those who WORK for them! There are no shortcuts, but, as I'll outline below, there are many things you can do to speed up the process, and make it easier.

✸ ✸ ✸

MANIFESTING 101

Here are the key concepts of manifesting as I know them. As time progresses, you will come up with your own techniques -- after all, we're not all wired the same way -- and I encourage you to experiment with these ideas as much as you can!

You get back what you give out

This is one of the truest statements I've ever known. As Louise L. Hay says, "The universe totally supports us in every thought we choose to think and believe." It is not choosy or picky: it will give you exactly what you wish for, consciously or unconsciously! On top of that, all your behaviour will circle back around to you. Are you loving and caring, or are you bossy and rigid? Do you share your life, your ideas, and your resources, or do you hold your cards close to your chest and block others out? Think about this when life doesn't seem to be delivering the results you might like. What have you been putting out into the universe?

Everything in your life is something that you want

This simple statement kicks up huge resistance for most people, which means it has struck a nerve. Why? Probably because most of us have things in our life which we are desperately unhappy with. That sucks, but don't despair. You don't have a miserable boyfriend because you consciously want that -- you have a miserable boyfriend because you crave it at an unconscious level. In the deepest recesses of your mind, you want him to reinforce your beliefs about men (that way, you never have to open up or make yourself vulnerable), or your subconscious wants to re-enact the relationship your parents had (to try and solve it once and for all), or you simply don't believe you deserve to have someone in your life who loves you and treats you like the babe you are.

We all have segments of our life which are tricky or don't seem to be working. Some of us have great fortune in relationships, but are always broke, for example. While these difficult issues can be great catalysts for growth, there is a reason why they are in our lives in the first place. See the next point!

Thoughts become things!

It is essential to remember that your feelings, not logic, create the conditions of your life! So if you feel muddled inside, don't be surprised when you open up your eyes to see a muddled existence. If you feel angry, you'll attract things into your existence to get angry about. On the other hand, if you feel good, loving, and magical, you'll attract good, loving, magical things. This really does work without fail. Thoughts become things is such an important piece of this puzzle!

Positive thoughts are much more powerful than negative thoughts

Don't worry: positive thoughts are much more powerful than negative ones! I know it's scary to hear that thoughts come things, especially if you watch the evening news, enjoy horror movies, or are a major worrywart! All is not lost, babe! Positive thoughts pack a walloping punch, and have way more juice and flavour than negative ones. While it's easy to get sucked into a negative thought, a good positive thought is like doing a seductive dance, all wrists and hips and gyrating pelvises! A positive thought starts small, teases a smile onto your face, and radiates out through your entire body. You tingle from your head to your toes and you are magnetic... and it's in this phase that wonderful things are attracted to you. They come shuttling towards you and want to attach themselves to your spirit!

You can use your feelings as a barometer

All of this good thought/bad thought stuff is enough to give any sane person a headache, but it's actually much easier than it sounds. You don't have to constantly patrol your thoughts like a jail warden. If you're concerned about what you might be attracting at any one time, just take a minute to take stock of how you feel inside. Are you feeling good? If so, great! You are attracting good things. If you're not feeling good, then you are attracting stuff you probably don't want. It's that simple. If you're not feeling good, do something to make yourself feel good!

You can change your negative feelings to positive feelings easily!

While most of us think we are not in control of our thoughts -- that they just happen to us -- this is untrue. While some of what we tell ourselves is unconscious, you can train yourself to be more positive. Learn to recognise when you're feeling bad or negative, and then figure out how to transform it. Usually, the best way to kick a feeling is to take action. The kind of action you take will depend on what's going on in your life. For example, running a quick mental list of ten things you're grateful for is a fantastic and easy way to spin a mood from dour to delightful. Singing, dancing, or exercising are three more great ways to change how you feel. This actually changes the chemistry in your brain! Give your dog a cuddle, call someone to tell them you love them, read one of your favourite poems... There are so many ways to make yourself feel good, and you can pick any of them!

In summary: if you're feeling bad, do something -- anything! -- to make you feel good.

Remember: your outcome depends on how you feel!

It's that easy, and that difficult. What does this tell you? It tells you that you should strive to be happy at all costs. If you feel that the circumstances of your life are conspiring to make you unhappy, then you need to take some action and switch it up, because no one else is going to do it for you! You need to take responsibility for your life and the direction it takes, because it is ALL YOU.

Know exactly what you want

As Steve Pavlina puts it, "Without a conscious intention, you're intending for the status quo to continue by default." If you don't know what you want, you'll get any old thing... And who wants that?

For some of us, it's difficult to work out what it is we REALLY want. We're so programmed by our parents, our lovers, our friends, the media, and society to place certain things on a pedestal and discard others. A lot of what we think we want from life comes from our background. If your parents took you to Europe during the school holidays, you probably think that is normal, and it is probably what you want for yourself and your family (if you have one). But if your parents expected you to get a job during the holidays, or if you all went and volunteered somewhere, then you probably think that is normal, too.

The reason I say this book is a primer on radical self love is because all of these concepts tie together. You'll notice echoes of other chapters within this chapter, and that's because no one piece of this ideology can work independently. You need all the puzzle pieces to come together in order to see results.

For example, you can't manifest a dream lover if you don't already love yourself (and therefore believe that you deserve perfect love). You won't be able to manifest anything meaningful if you refuse to take responsibility for your life and your choices, because your head wouldn't be in the right place -- and if you did somehow create something special, you'd probably just chalk it up to "luck"! Further to that, if you don't take responsibility and your attempts at manifesting wonderful things fall flat, you'd be quick to dismiss it all as hocus-pocus bullshit, rather than thinking there was something you could have done to make it better!

The best place to start is by taking responsibility for your life once and for all. It is from that feeling of complete control that you can start to plant the seeds which will bring it all together.

HOW TO WORK OUT WHAT YOU REALLY WANT

The media is constantly selling us these objects of aspiration and telling us how to live our lives, and it's such bullshit! Do you really want a new Mercedes-Benz and a boob job? Do you really want a child and a wedding ring? Do you really want your own private jet? Some people discover that yes, they DO want these things after lots of soul-searching, and some uncover the opposite. What you truly desire for your life is probably wildly different to what you think it is. You can live however you want, truly. If you threw off all the shackles that society wanted to put on you, where would it leave you?

Do you really want a brand new condo, or would you prefer to ride trains across the country? Do you really want a husband or wife, or would you prefer to take a series of lovers? Do you really want to work for someone else, or do you want to strike out on your own?

It's time to actually think about what you want. One of the best ways to do this is to disconnect from the internet, television and radio for a couple of days. It's hard to get attuned to your true self when you have a slew of loud voices yelling at you, telling you what to do all the time! Meditate. Go for a walk. Have a swim. Look through your closet. Get a massage. Examine the stuff you have on your walls: what is it saying? Does it really represent you?

Grab a piece of paper and start to plot out what you think you want. It's okay to write things which contradict one another, because when you start this process your mind will go in different directions for a while. As you move through it, your mind will become clearer, and the things which actually thrill you will jump out at you like big shiny gems. The more you think about it, the more obvious it will become.

It is really just a case of devoting some time to it and spending some time with your thoughts, which so few of us do! When was the last time you were alone and thinking, without having a book, a movie, the television, a magazine or a playlist to distract you?

The more time you spend thinking deeply, the more in-tune with yourself you will be.

Once you get clear on these things, you can start to create the life of your dreams.

MAKING IT HAPPEN

Once your piece of paper is starting to look really appealing to you, gear up your life and environment so that it supports you. After all, it's hard to make magic when your bedroom looks like a bomb hit it, and your life is a trainwreck!

Clear out the clutter and mess

When's the last time you gave your house or bedroom a deep clean? Now is the time! Get rid of -- or put into storage -- the things that don't support you in your mission. This may mean taking down photos of ex-lovers, getting rid of pictures which don't inspire you, and deleting numbers from your phone! As well as the physical mess which may surround you (piles of unfiled papers, dirty socks, etc.), there are lots of things we all hold on to which take up emotional, mental or psychic space, often without us realising. It is so empowering to create a blank slate and start fresh. The more you clear out your space, the better you'll feel.

Replace the old clutter with totems and power items

My definition of a power item is something which inspires you or reminds you of what you're aiming for! When I started writing about radical self love, one of the first tasks I set was for everyone to get their hands on a radical self love totem. I wanted all my readers to have something nearby which reminded them of what they were striving for, which was ultimate self-love! My radical self love totem was a huge heart-shaped necklace covered in sparkly Swarovski crystals. Wearing it every day and seeing it in the mirror reminded me of what I was striving for.

Why not fill your room with images of what you want, Post-It Notes which say "YES!" and things which make you feel good to look at them? Stack your bookshelves with books that inspire you to be your best self. Stock your fridge with food which makes you feel healthy and energised. Hang a pirate flag if that inspires you! There is no right or wrong; use your internal compass to guide you.

Write down what you want

Make a list, and write it in the present tense. Start with, "I am so happy and grateful…" and then fill in the blank.

I am so happy and grateful that I am getting healthier every day. I am so happy and grateful that I am in a loving, respectful, and fun relationship. I am so happy and grateful that my business is earning more money than ever before. I am so happy and grateful that I am going to the Bahamas this year for a relaxing holiday with my wife!

Be specific. Use words which have energy and meaning to you! Remember, you are writing this for yourself, so make it fun to read. It should be the sort of thing you want to look at often, because it boosts your energy and makes you feel good.

Keep this piece of paper within an easy line of sight. That way you will be constantly reminded of what you want, as well as giving you access to it so you can alter it, add to it, and adjust it to suit you as you grow. My list is in my Filofax, in front of my to do list, and behind a tarot card of The High Priestess! For me the placement is perfect, and every time I look it, it fills me with inspiration, happiness and hope.

Make a vision board

I'm big on visuals, and I like to collect inspiration wherever I go. For example, I have six clipboards above my desk which I like to load up with images to keep me invigorated and excited about life!

Make your own vision boards, either on clipboards or a bulletin board. It's so easy to do: just grab a stack of magazines and start tearing out pages. Pull out anything that catches your eye and is in alignment with the life you want to create. Then, get artistic and arrange them on the board before pinning, clipping, or washi taping them in place.

Having a visual representation of your goals is so motivating, and it's yet another way to fill your mind with positive ideas and images. Remember, thoughts become things!

Write affirmations

Tailor them to your situation, and put them somewhere that you'll see them all the time! Say them out loud regularly, although, like me, you might be too embarrassed to do this at first. That's okay: just read them a lot!

Make your affirmations fun. Write them in lipstick on your mirror, or put them on Post-It notes and dot them around your house.

Learn to visualise what you want

Our subconscious doesn't work with words, it works with pictures and feelings. Every thought you think is like a tiny movie being projected across your brain, saturating your subconscious. The more clearly you can see something in your mind, the more real it will become. I believe that you cannot do something in your physical body until you have done it in your head first.

Create a movie in your head of the things you want, and play it all the time. Get fully immersed in the experience -- don't just watch it passively, allow yourself to feel the rush of emotions that would whizz by if this was happening right now, in real life! This should be exhilarating, you should love doing it and relish every moment. If it isn't, maybe you're visualising something you're not truly passionate about. Back to the drawing board with you!

Act "as if"

Like attracts like. If you behave as if what you want has already happened, it will come to you more readily. Some of this operates on a kooky, metaphysical level, but the rest of it is total logic. For example, if you dress like you're part of the management team, they'll be more likely to promote you, since you already look like you fit in. If you're responsible with your money, you'll become wealthier. You get the gist!

When it comes to manifesting something you want, do your best to act as if you already have it. At first, you might feel like a big phony because clearly you don't have those things yet, but you need to fool yourself anyway. Act as if you have that thing. Act as if it's on loan. Act as if the cheque's in the mail. Act as if you know it's just around the corner. Act this way with your whole being, from the way that you walk, to the way that you dress, and the way that you talk. (This having been said, don't break the bank on appearances. It's more about the feeling, and the emotions around that, than how you actually look. You'll get what I mean if you give it a try.)

Devote time to making magic

If you don't commit to making time for manifesting, it can easily slide to the bottom of your to do list. Even if you use 15 minutes on the bus in the morning to close your eyes and visualise all the things you want, it will make a HUGE difference.

Take time to read books on self-improvement, to visualise, to work on your vision board. Make a commitment to speaking positively and kindly. Write a gratitude list first thing every morning. Make these things part of your life and routine. If they don't drastically alter your life, I will eat my hat!

Remember that you can predict your future by assessing your thoughts!

You can tell how happy your life will be in the near future by paying attention to your thoughts. Of course, if you are complaining or constantly negative, that indicates you're not very happy (and that your future will follow suit), but I've learned that even if I'm spending a lot of time reminiscing about the past, something is amiss. Why should I be hankering over the past when I have this perfectly good life right here, right now?

If you find yourself complaining and grizzling all the time, launch a "no complaining" rule. See how long you can go without speaking badly about anyone or anything. Encourage your friends to join in, too!

You don't need to see the whole path in order to make things happen

You really don't. The path will unfold as you continue walking. This can be scary, especially for those of us who love to plan and like to be in charge. But when it comes to working with the universe, thinking that you know exactly how things should play out will only do you a disservice.

You see, manifesting is an imprecise art. It's partly knowing what you want, but it's also partly getting out of the way and allowing the universe to work its magic. You need to let go of thinking you know the best way for things to happen, because even though we think we have all the answers, we don't!

Sure, you might know the best place to get a deal on designer shoes, or the best company to call to move your furniture, but when it comes to manifesting things, you need to back off. Just state what you want, and then get out of the way. Don't you think the universe knows best? It does. If you don't believe this, you'll be beaten over the head repeatedly until you do!

Don't be attached to what you want

This can be the trickiest part. After all, if you want something, it makes sense to be attached to that desire. The key, though, is to know what you want, take some action (by writing it down, making a vision board, or visualising it every morning), and then letting it go. Trust that it will show up when you need it!

You have to have faith in the process, and trust that it's working. This requires patience. It's impossible to say how long it will take for something to manifest or happen, it's like asking about the length of a piece of string. It could happen immediately, or it could take three months. But you need to keep the faith. Continue taking action and moving forward.

So often, someone will decide to give manifesting a shot. They'll make the vision board, do the exercises, and strive to be positive, but after a couple of weeks, can't see any progress. They inevitably start to doubt the process. They say, "Ahh, this is stupid! It doesn't work!" Of course, the universe hears you, and does what you ask: it takes it all away.

Learn to ask for what you want

People who don't ask for things don't get them. Period. Again, another old saying comes to mind: "You miss 100% of the shots you don't take."

Most of us aren't very good at asking for help, even though we all need it! It's a curse of modern life: we feel like we should be able to do everything on our own, and that to admit otherwise is a sign of weakness.

If this is resonating with you, don't be so silly! I promise that it will take you much longer to get things done if you obstinately insist on doing everything by yourself! Please reach out to the people around you. The worst they can say is "No", and then you're no worse off than when you started! Take a load off, and ask for help... Often!

Embrace change

If you want change, but you're also afraid of it, you're in for a rough ride. When the first teeny tiny seedlings of change start to poke their heads through the earth, your anxiety will hit the roof, and prevent good things from happening.

Learn to get down with change, to embrace it and welcome it in, even to do a victory dance when you see it crossing your threshold, because it will be your salvation. When you see things changing, you know your life is improving. It means that the universe has perked up its ears and is listening and whispering back, and that all the things you've been waiting for are coming to you!

It can take time to get comfortable with the concept of change, especially if you prefer to cling to the familiar, but it's worth settling into. Breathe into it like a good, deep yoga pose. The real truth of it is that life is changing all the time, and it doesn't really care what your thoughts are on the matter. You can love it or hate it, and life will change all the same. If you can get cozy with the concept of change, however, life moves much more smoothly, things will unfold with grace, and you can accept the new parts of your life with a smile.

Whatever you resist persists, and whatever you're thinking about will come about. If you're constantly thinking, "I don't want things to change", whoosh! Change comes rushing towards you. So by resisting change, you are really bringing heaps of it into your life before you're prepared for it. Just one more reason to settle into change, and learn to love it!

Remember that possessions will not make you happy

Actually, it works in reverse! Being happy is what allows you to attract the things you want! Once you are happy, satisfied, and in love with yourself, you will notice that life gets exponentially better every day. All those things you wanted will start to appear in your life. Getting happy is the first step, and the most crucial one. So many people think that they will be happy once they have a house, a car, a husband, a baby, and the list goes on. It doesn't work like that.

Material possessions, relationships or children will never plug that gap inside of you. Only you can do that for yourself. It's something we have to figure out on our own, and sometimes we only work it out when we're really at our wit's end.

When it comes to creating the life of your dreams, the key is to simply begin.

There are no perfect moments, and there is no ideal time. There is an old proverb which says, "The best time to plant a tree is twenty years ago. The second best time is now", and it couldn't be more applicable. There's no point in despairing over what you have or haven't done. Whatever the reason -- whether you didn't have enough information, or didn't have the right motivation, or weren't ready yet -- it is entirely irrelevant. That time has passed, it is gone, you will never get it back. Regret is a waste of energy, and regret never achieves anything. The very best thing to do is keep looking towards the sky, be smart and strategic, and do what you need to do today to ensure a glorious future.

Always remember that the way you feel is a preview of what's coming. If you don't feel good, do something to make you feel good!

Learning how to manifest the best life ever isn't about sitting around, being faux-positive, and living in denial. Good things come to those who work for them!

#RSLBOOK

HOMEWORK

❤ FIGURE OUT WHAT YOU REALLY WANT.

Disconnect from the internet for a couple of days and spend some time getting reacquainted with yourself. It's time to discover what you want from your life, and if you don't make time to do it now, when will you?

❤ WRITE DOWN WHAT YOU WANT.

Once you've figured out at least a few things you know you want, write it all down. Remember to write it in the present tense. Visualise it as you write it. Infuse the words with feeling and emotion! It should feel really good when you re-read it.

❤ CREATE A VISION BOARD.

It's time to get crafty! Use clippings from magazines and print-outs from Pinterest to create a visual representation of what you want in your life. It will keep you motivated when you feel stuck, and remind you of where you're heading.

❤ DO WHATEVER YOU NEED TO DO TO FEEL GOOD.

Really, one of the most important things you can do is focus on feeling good, because when you feel good, you'll attract good things. It sounds deceptively simple, I know, but give it a shot!

❤ ACT "AS IF"!

Always act "as if" whatever you want to manifest has already happened. Behave the way someone with that career, income, or relationship would behave. Catch your physical self up to your emotional self!

STYLE IS HOW YOU LIVE YOUR LIFE

A deluxe guide to looking fabulous,
defining your personal style, and being
the best-dressed babe at any party!

WHY STYLE IS IMPORTANT

Style permeates everything you do. In fact, style is not just what you wear, but how you live your life!

Firstly, let's look at why style is important in the first place, or why it's worth talking about. After all, style is not essential. There are plenty of people whose lives are mostly devoid of (intentional) beauty, who couldn't care less about what they're wearing, and their lives seem to be going off without a hitch. They have jobs, houses, cars, families, friends, and they manage to exist like anybody else.

However, some of us are wired a little differently. I am an appreciator of beauty, and I suspect you are too. You probably know, like I do, that a life lived with style is so very satisfying. We are all familiar with the effect that a piece of art, or a particular song, or a well-written book can have on us. It brings us so much delight, and so much pleasure.

It sounds overly simplistic, but a wonderful coat or a fabulous hat enhances life, and makes it much more beautiful. You can see this very clearly in television and movies: a good storyline is made even better by clever styling and strong aesthetics. Styling can add layers, depth, and complexity. Clothing conveys mood and intentions, and can even betray secrets.

We all know that style intensifies our experience of life, but putting that into practice can prove a little trickier. A lot of us default to wearing a kind of uniform every day, because the thought of busting through a sartorial rut seems so difficult. When our boots finally fall apart, or a massive hole appears in a favourite sweater, we often go out and replace it with exactly the same thing. Our inner self may have evolved, but our outer self hasn't changed so much as a pair of socks!

It's one thing to know what you like, and in fact, that is wonderful. But it's another to stick to the tried-and-true because we don't know how to express ourselves any other way.

Unravelling and discovering your personal style goes hand-in-hand with discovering yourself. Our internal (emotional, mental, and spiritual) world is inherently linked to our external one. We can express how we feel on the inside by showing it in how we are dressed. We can use clothing to express ourselves and send a message to the world. The message could be anything, from "Don't mess with me" to "I'd rather be climbing trees" to "#1 Kevin Spacey fan"!

Sometimes we do this without meaning to, on a subconscious level.

What did you wear yesterday? What were you thinking as you got dressed? Now, step outside of yourself for a moment, and consider what that ensemble said about you to people on the street. Did it say, "I have three children and a full-time job"? Did it say, "I hate everyone"? Did it say, "I am a powerful, magical glamazon"?

How do you feel about conveying that message? Does it make you feel good, or would you prefer to be communicating something else?

As we discussed earlier, first impressions count, and our clothes make up around 50% of that first impression. No matter how many times we're told not to judge a book by its cover, we still do. It is human nature, and we use this information to determine our initial thoughts about a person.

This is not to say you have to play it safe and dull -- not at all. Someone who looks a bit wacky, but is clearly having fun with clothing, is one of my favourite things to see. I enjoy those looks a lot more than the flawlessly-styled girls strolling down Park Avenue, because being perfectly appropriate can be so boring! A little bit of bad taste is good for you. Being conservative lacks a certain spark.

Christian Dior once said that zest was the secret of all beauty, and

I love that! I agree 100%: all great style and beauty has an element of zest. Zest is utterly personal: it is a form of individuation. It has something that leaps out at you, something that makes an impact. It doesn't have to roar or be totally ostentatious. It can be as flashy as a beautiful ring, or as subtle as a sparkle in the eye. But there has to be something that makes what you're wearing totally yours, some way of personalising the ensemble so that it's fun, delicious, original, and quintessentially you.

Two women wearing the same dress can look completely different. Part of this is anatomy, since your body type is always going to change the way a dress looks, but part of it is in the accessories.

Think about the LBD (Little Black Dress) made famous by Coco Chanel. She always said that every woman should have an LBD which is perfect for all occasions, and of course, most women do. The thing that differentiates every woman in an LBD at a party is the way it's styled. Some girls will team it with heels and a pair of diamond earrings. Another girl might pair it with a wonderful hat and jangling bracelets. Again, it is about your zest, your style, your flair.

Society would love to have us feel bad, guilty, and unhappy about the way we look: it's good for big business, pumping us full of sugar-free food, and encouraging us to trot off to the surgeon at a moment's notice. But my advice is to ignore all of that, and dress to make yourself happy.

Some people won't like the way you dress, but that is the way it goes. Everyone has different taste, and your ensemble is never going to be a smash hit across the globe. Some people think that you MUST dress to hide your lumps and bumps. Others think shape be damned, I want colour! Plenty of people just want to look interesting, and are not all that concerned about anything else. Some are obsessed with labels while others will never buy anything new. Think about the multitude of diverse looks you see in your city every day. We all have very individual tastes and beliefs about style. No one way of thinking is right or wrong.

I like to simplify the whole subject by using this as my guiding principle: if I feel good in it, the outfit is a success.

You have to work with what you've got, and dress to show off your best attributes. Wishin' and hopin' and prayin' that you'll wake up and be 5'10" is a waste of time and energy, because no matter how high your heels (or how tight your compression underpants!), you are who you are.

Dress to make yourself happy, rather than attempting to chase perfection all the time. You will never get there, and there is no such thing as flawlessness. Confidence comes from feeling good in your clothing, and if you do, you'll have a much better time than the girl who looks immaculate but is freaked out in the corner.

Remember that making mistakes is part of the deal! Fashion faux pas and not-so-fabulous moments happen to everyone, from the avid risk-takers to the jeans-and-T-shirt set, so just accept them as being par for the course.

A wonderful way to chart your sartorial progress is to take daily outfit photos. They have real, practical application, like, for example, being able to look at your outfit and know whether it was a hit or a miss. It's easier to be objective when looking at a photo (rather than in a mirror), and it's also a handy reference for your favourite outfits. This can really speed things up when you're in a rush!

Remember that exploring your style takes time. It is a continual and evolving process. You will find bits that work, while the rest continues to change. Maybe your haircut is ideal or you know what shape suits you best, but the rest of it is in flux. That's great: it's good to have elements which anchor your look while you experiment with the rest.

Getting dressed should be an enjoyable process, and to help facilitate that, we're going to come up with a bunch of ways for you to feel really good about clothing on a daily basis!

* * *

MY STYLE EVOLUTION

Like every woman, I have had moments of fashion brilliance and moments of sartorial despair. It is a learning process and it never really ends. You have to make mistakes to discover what works, so don't beat yourself up, just laugh and move on!

I grew up in the back of my mother's clothing boutique. As well as becoming extremely familiar with Frank Sinatra's entire discography, I learned a lot about clothing just from what I heard on the other side of the door. I would hear women refusing to try things on in size x, because their vanity wouldn't allow it. I heard the exclaims of delight as women tried on colours they had never previously considered. I discovered that every woman's individual relationship to clothing and personal expression was complicated, and that life was too short to wear something you didn't love.

At school, I wore a uniform, which was an endless source of frustration. I was keen on expressing myself, and because I had to wear the same thing every day, I wasn't able to. Our uniform code was extremely strict: we were told off for having our shirts untucked, for shortening our skirts (which were supposed to hit unflatteringly below-the-knee), and for wearing make-up or nail polish. In fact, if you were wearing nail polish, they would send you to the office where you would have to pay 50 cents to use their bottle of acetone to remove it! Jewellery was confiscated without a second thought, hair had to be cut short or tied up, and we even had regulation hair-ties. It was oppressive to the extreme, and it felt like torture every day. However, the silver lining in all of this is that I'm sure it motivated me to become the person I am today. Maybe if I had been able to dress however I liked, I wouldn't now feel driven to dress up and express myself through clothing the way I do.

My first real foray into dressing the way I wanted to was by jumping head-first into all things dark and wonderful. I Was A Teenage Goth, oh yes. I dyed my bob blue-black, I wore black and white striped stockings and long black skirts, I owned a fantastic corset and yes, I rocked an ankh necklace. The first pair of shoes I really lusted after were a pair of New Rock boots. I bought them in 1996, at age 13. I vividly remember my father telling me how hideous they were, and of course, that cemented their place in my heart forever. Other than school shoes, I really did not wear anything but my New Rocks until I was about 20 years old. I even wore them with my suit to my first ever job... in a bank!

My goth phase lasted until I was in my early 20s. I only wore black. I considered a spiked dog collar to be essential jewellery. I lived with a guy who wore buckled PVC pants on the weekend. Oh, what a world! Finally, I broke up with that boyfriend and moved out on my own, and the way I dressed started to change.

Living by myself, I began to really explore who I was, and went through a stage of huge personal growth. As part of this, I started to experiment with colour. I bought my first pair of blue jeans. I wore duck-egg blue cowboy boots with shredded silk dresses, I layered cardigans and beads, and I donned enormous sunglasses. I went crazy on accessories. I started to show my legs for the first time, which was previously something I never, ever did.

My style has continued to evolve since then. I have toned down the extreme colour, which I am sure was just a reaction to years of wearing black and nothing else. I love a punchy hue, but not from head-to-toe!

I'm most comfortable in black ankle boots or sneaker wedges. I love short skirts with graphic tees, bright dresses, and bold jewellery. I am very fond of using humour in the way I dress, too, by wearing a pair of leather bunny ears or a big flower crown.

Style is about proportion and contrast. I love to wear a voluminous tutu skirt with boots, a sequin miniskirt with a slouchy t-shirt, or a pair of oversized glasses with a cocktail dress. All of my favourite outfits have some element of surprise. Sometimes it works, and sometimes it doesn't, but that's all part of the adventure!

If I had to describe my look, I would call it Eccentric Pop. It's Sunday best on acid. It has taken me a long time to get to this point, but it makes me really happy.

✳ ✳ ✳

SETTING LIMITS: HOW THEY CAN HELP YOU

When it comes to dressing yourself, the sky's the limit -- but sometimes that simple fact can be intimidating in and of itself. If you can go in any direction, how do you know where to begin?! In this scenario, it can help to be aware of some vital pieces of information.

Sit down and consider the following. (How much you let these aspects affect you is entirely up to you, but they will all impact on your look to varying degrees.)

The colours which suit you

While a lot of style guides would have you chuck on any old colour, I don't believe that is the best way of doing things. We all have a personal palette of colours which make us look dazzling, and a smattering of colours which makes us look like we have the plague. Unless zombie chic is your chosen style expression, these colours are best avoided! If you know what colours flatter you, that will really help you when you go shopping, and you'll also be able to steer clear of enormous sections of the store!

Your lifestyle

If you're a personal trainer with three children, the way you dress yourself will be very different to a socialite's daily garb. People living in Alaska have entirely different sartorial needs to those living in Fiji, Mormons don't usually dress like atheists, and every culture has its own traditions that we choose to either adhere to or ignore. This is without even considering which subcultural groups you may consider yourself a member of, and their various rules or guidelines on dress.

Additionally, while you may be the most liberated person on the planet, what you wear will naturally change depending on the situation and location. For example, I know that an outfit that will net me concerned stares in New Zealand will not even warrant a second look in New York City!

On top of all of this, there are some countries where showing even the tiniest hint of skin is horribly offensive. So your day-to-day activities, occupation, romantic life and general living situation will definitely dictate some elements of your style.

Your budget

Sad, but true. We can't all dress head to toe in Saint Laurent, and so this influences our choices too. For most of us, keeping a roof overhead is the most important thing, and so despite all our lust over a pair of designer kicks, the majority of our money tends to go towards something more practical.

That's okay, though. A lot of people get tricked into thinking that just because something was expensive, it's automatically better, and this is simply not true. Having a lot of money at your disposal can actually make people a little bit lazy about how they get dressed and what they wear. Just because your outfit cost as much as 3 months rent for the girl standing next to you, you don't necessarily have more style than she does. In fact, if it's not put together well, it just makes you a fool in expensive duds! Fact. You can see this all over the place: celebrities with more money than God can't seem to pull an outfit together, and most of them even have stylists that they pay to do it for them!

Don't let the fact that you have real fiscal responsibilities make you feel like looking good or being well-dressed is out of your reach, because it's not. When you're short on cash, you're forced to innovate, and that's where the real magic and wonder comes into the equation. I adore mixing high- and low-end together; I think it makes fashion so much more fun, and it gives me a huge thrill to be able to tell someone who likes my dress that I scored it for less than $50 just down the street! All of this to say, yes, you need to be aware of your budget, but don't see it as a limiting factor. Just use it as fuel to do bigger and better things!

Your body

It just makes sense that a 6' woman and a 4' woman will have very different wardrobes, and not only because of their individual tastes, but because of what looks good and flattering on them. You can look incredible regardless of your height or your size, but you do need to be conscious of it so that you can make informed choices. If you're straight up and down and you wear shapeless dresses, it's not going to do a lot for you. But if you play it up with colour and proportion, you'll look much more ravishing. The more you experiment, the better you will become at dressing for your shape.

Your age

It makes me nuts when I read something which says you basically have to be invisible at age 40, especially since I know I'm going to be there one day myself and dressing to be invisible is totally NOT on my personal agenda! However, there is something to be said for mothers and daughters not wearing the exact same outfit to the movies. As you get older, it is natural and normal for your style of dress to change. Your style should evolve, just like everything else! It's not about hiding yourself away or not having fun, it's about knowing who you are, and growing into that role comfortably and with grace.

Similarly, it wigs me out when young teenage girls dress like 35 year old women. I think an important component of personal style is being able to appreciate who you are in this moment, and never pretending to be someone else.

Your rules

Where do you draw the line? We all have ideas about what we will and will not do, and this extends to how we dress. Do you wear glasses all the time? How do you feel about wearing fur? Are you vegan? How do you feel about "fast fashion"? Do leggings or ugg boots have their place in your wardrobe?

All of these things will influence the way you dress and the facets of appearance that you're likely to explore. If you're vegan with a fetish for crazy sunglasses, that gives you some very defined and specific criteria to work with.

Sometimes, the idea of setting limits makes us nervous, but actually, knowing what you're okay with just makes it easier to be creative.

Having said that, I think we can never say never. I was once given a pair of ugg boots (after secretly loathing them for years), and now I am a total convert. My God, are they comfortable!

✳ ✳ ✳

HOW TO DEVELOP YOUR OWN STYLE

When it comes to being successful at anything, experimentation is the key. Try, try again; fail quickly and move on. You have to try new things so that you know what works and what doesn't! It just makes sense: the more information you have on a subject, the better you are at making choices. With clothing, there are so many variables that trying a lot of different options will help you build up a firm idea of your true taste.

Find your style icons and inspirations

If you're only now feeling the need to crawl out of your blue jean coma, it can be very daunting. How the hell are you supposed to know what to buy? Do you just run into the closest shop, buy a bunch of stuff and hope for the best? Well, you could, but I don't recommend it. The best way to do it is to look at people who you think have exemplary style, and use what they have learned as a guide. Watch, observe, and replicate. Why reinvent the wheel?

Your inspirations can come from anywhere, there are no restrictions! You could be invigorated by the colours of the postman's uniform, transfixed by the sparkles along a drag queen's eyelids, or fall head-over-heels for an old photograph of Betsey Johnson. It doesn't matter what it is, just as long as it provides something delicious for your soul and your imagination to feast on!

Start a style bible

The best way to do this is to buy a big blank hardcover book with lots of pages, and treat it like your very own aesthetic bible. Moleskine make my favourite notebooks, and their big, hardcover, A4-sized books are totally ideal for this purpose.

You can put anything in here that you choose, but a good place to start is by writing down your style history. This could mean reminiscing about your favourite dresses, thinking about what your mother wore when she went out on the town, remembering how a certain make-up artist painted you up one time, or writing a long love letter to all the shoes you never bought! Stick in photographs of your best (and worst) fashion moments. Think about what inspires you, and consider your biggest and most successful sartorial risks. Write about your friends' looks, dissect what makes them work, and think about how you could bring some of their flair into your wardrobe. Jot down any ideas you have, stick in pictures, make lists of items you want, and plot outfits.

Doing this will jolt you awake to your own ideas about look, aesthetics, fashion and style. After all, if you don't think about something very often, you're unlikely to have an opinion on the subject! It will begin to give you a place to begin, and you'll realise all the possibilities and options you can explore. When it comes to style, nothing is off-limits, and experimenting with it on paper is a great way of discovering that.

Host a style swap

If you have stylish friends, this is worth doing! All you need are a few willing participants, some champagne (just for fun), and a location!

The recipe is simple: everyone brings a few pieces that they don't wear anymore, and -- as the name would imply -- swap! If swapping clothes makes you feel anxious, how about limiting it to accessories, just to start? Hopefully you will all end up with a couple of nice new-to-you pieces, but if not, it's not the end of the world... At least you got to spend time with your friends!

Take photos of your outfits

I have been talking about the value of daily outfit photos since 2006. If you're not taking photos of your outfits yet, you should seriously think about doing so. You don't have to put them on the internet, either -- just do it for your own reference.

Take a series of pictures: front, back and side are most helpful when it comes to assessing how you look. Very few of us even know what we look like from the back, so this can be a real eye-opener!

Save all of these pictures onto your computer, organise them into a folder, label them chronologically (sorry, sometimes I cannot suppress my inner Virgo!), and then look them over. Make notes if you want. Think about how the outfit could have been improved. You will learn so much about aesthetics and more specifically, what it takes to make your body look its best, through doing this.

You will begin to notice small things, like the fact that wherever there is a horizontal line (from a belt, or the top of a sock, or an ankle-strap on a shoe), you look wider. You'll see the difference between how your legs look in white stockings versus black. You'll get a much more realistic view of what your best assets are, and how to dress them so they look stupendous. You will realise the difference good underwear makes. You will learn what length of skirt is most flattering on you, which necklines suit you and what kind of sleeve is most flattering, and as you discover these things, your confidence will grow.

Make vision or inspiration boards

You can buy a huge cork bulletin board from any stationery store for practically nothing. Whenever you see something in a magazine that you want to emulate or try out, tear it out and stick it up. It could be anything, from an entire outfit to a tiny detail -- the way someone wears a belt, a pair of stockings, or even a visual depiction of a mood. Hang the board on the wall next to your closet, and look at it when you're getting dressed. This helps so much with not getting sick of your wardrobe and giving you new ideas for wearing old things that you would not believe it.

The best thing about a bulletin or cork board is that it can be changed instantly, which is great for fickle or over-imaginative minds!

Use a wardrobe app

The future is so cool. One of my favourite iPhone apps is called Stylebook, and you use it to take photos of all the items in your closet. Then you can drag them around to make virtual outfits! It's brilliant, very Cher Horowitz from Clueless. It also helps you to see at a glance exactly what you own!

With an app like Stylebook, you can even recreate outfits you've worn in the past that you deemed as being particularly successful. Make notes as to how it could be modified, or add different belts and accessories that you think could enhance the outfit in the future.

This kind of thing can be a neverending project, which is really what style is all about. While fashion is something that constantly changes and is dictated to us by magazines, style is not. It has very strong roots, but the best style evolves.

Remember that nothing has to be permanent

A lot of us are intimidated by the idea of putting a stake in the ground and saying, "This is my style, and I stand by it forever!" In fact, it would be weird to stick to the same thing forever. It's totally normal, and even encouraged, for our style to change constantly.

Don't feel like you have to commit to anything forever. If you can view your path of personal style growth as an evolution, something which is fluid and mercurial and prone to flights of fancy, it will take a lot of the anxiety out of it.

Make an effort

Finally, and perhaps most importantly, it helps to make an effort. All the theoretical knowledge in the world won't make an inch of difference if you don't take it and actually apply it in the real world! Make notes on things you would like to try or improve upon -- anything from trying a new foundation to pairing high heels with an unexpected outfit -- and then act on them!

It feels good to be all dolled up. When you think back on your most wonderful moments, odds are excellent that they were times when you had made the effort to get dressed up for some kind of occasion, as opposed to running down to the shops in your baggy leggings! While you don't have to spend three hours making up your face every morning, just spending a little extra time on your presentation will make you feel so much better and more confident about how you look! Even an awesome pair of sneakers worn with a bright lip will add excitement to your step and give you a little boost.

Hard work is always rewarded, and that applies to everything. If you put extra energy into the way you look, it will pay dividends!

INSPIRATION IS EVERYWHERE

I am inspired by the whole world. From Pee-Wee Herman to psychedelic starscapes, marabou-draped models to couples in love, from multi-coloured cowboy boots to perfect retro pin-ups... They all tickle different parts of my brain, and make me want to try new things. I don't necessarily want to emulate what I've seen, but I'm itching to invoke that same mood or give off a similar kind of attitude.

That's the thing about inspiration: it should be an homage rather than a straight-up impersonation. Otherwise, you might as well be going to a costume party. The idea is to take something someone has done and either improve on it or personalise it so that it is more tailored to you and your style. This is not weird or sneaky, it is just the way of the world. Everyone borrows from everyone else. Being a carbon copy is to be avoided, however: that's just like a big blinking sign above your forehead which says, "I have no thoughts of my own!"

If you're unsure of where to start garnering style inspiration, do a little internet exploration and you will surely turn up plenty of wonderful things. Pinterest is great for this, a total treasure trove!

I find most of my inspiration in the wild people from history. After all, people have had to dress themselves since the dawn of time, and plenty of them did it extremely well! Some style icons through the ages include Coco Chanel (her androgynous, relaxed look and clean palettes are emulated to this day), Little Edie (of Grey Gardens fame), Edie Sedgwick (Andy Warhol's muse and revolutionary dresser), Isabella Blow (always wore a hat and lipstick), Jackie Onassis (inspired a generation of women to dress up), Dita Von Teese (brought back glamour and pin-up style), Gwen Stefani (always takes risks while maintaining a signature look), Diana Vreeland (loved red and thought about fashion in an entirely original way), Marilyn Monroe (the original sex symbol), Audrey Hepburn (showed how alluring grace really was), Kate Moss (always ahead of trends and a true trailblazer), Carrie

Bradshaw (fictional but brilliant), and the list goes on...

You don't have to go for the tried and true or even well-known. Looking through photos from historical archives can turn up all kinds of treasures. Anywhere that interesting people congregated can be great for super-inspiring, investigative research. Just think about the looks at Woodstock, or the people who dwelled in the Hotel Chelsea. How about the early punks in London, or 1950s youth? Harajuku in Tokyo is known for some of the most colourful, exciting ensembles in a long time. While it may not be in your budget to go and investigate these areas in person, so much can be gleaned from books, shrewd internet searches, and talking to people who were there at the time.

Be an unabashed aesthetics thief. Take everything that appeals to you, or speaks to you, or makes you think of something brilliant, and put it all together in one place. Stick it into your style bible, pin it to your vision board, use it to assemble outfits of your own, even tape the pictures to the headboard of your bed to inspire yummy, stylish dreams! (Some of my best outfits have come to me in dreams!) Don't be afraid to use anything and everything in your quest to make your life more beautiful in every way.

✳ ✳ ✳

PUTTING IT ALL TOGETHER

There are no rules, despite what some of those dreadful television shows might say. There are only ideas to try, so here are a few to chew over!

Remember that you do not have to stick to one look or style. That's just dressing by numbers! Quelle yawn! Why not combine elements of grunge (flannel shirts, ripped jeans, babydoll dresses), new wave (wild eye make-up, striped t-shirts, rubber bracelets), rave (bright colours, childlike jewellery, body glitter), goth (black, crucifixes, texture, dark make-up), punk (Doc Martens, zippers, studs) and pin-up (suspender belts, back-seamed stockings, red lipstick)? Fill your closet with fantastic things which thrill you. Buy turbans, fluffy faux-fur coats, fetish shoes, sunglasses of every shape for every foreseeable mood, sequins, huge earrings, silk scarves, and perfectly-tailored dresses. Wear a tuxedo, a casual full-length dress, a cape, a leather jacket. Add fresh flowers to your hair, wear more than one watch at a time, buy a pair of fingerless leather gloves in a shocking hue. Collect vintage brooches, interesting glasses, tiaras. Wear ruffles, prints, shaggy fur, fringe!

Surprise yourself. Use every situation as an opportunity to try something new stylistically. If it's really terrible, you can always run home again! It is never as much of a crisis as you think it is.

Think about balance and proportion. Fashion is about architecture after all! If you're in a voluminous skirt, keep it closely-tailored up top. Conversely, if you're in a loose, drapey shirt, try a pair of skinny pants or a short skirt. Always go for the contrast. If you're wearing an elaborate dress, keep your hair simple. If you're wearing red lipstick, tone down the rest of your make-up. You get the idea. Try mixing clichés, or wearing total opposites. How about a floral dress with a motorcycle jacket?

Where can you create shape, add dimension, or create a kind of optical illusion with your look? Maybe an A-line skirt worn with heels will make your legs look ultra-long, or a cardigan cinched in with a thin yellow belt will give you a fabulous waist. Make your hair big and puffy; pull it back and wear it off your face. Wear a huge necklace or a super-fine chain. Examine the way patterns and prints brighten or dull your complexion. (Sometimes this can be hard to assess in a mirror, so take photos instead.)

Choose one element to play up, and take it from there. Maybe it's a sequin bolero, perhaps it's an incredible pair of shoes. Allow that item to be the feature focus, and pull back the rest of your look accordingly. As fun as it can be to look like a disco ball (sometimes!), it can be much more chic to show a little restraint.

Mix it up. Pair vintage with high-end -- like a well-worn velvet blazer with a crisp new sundress -- or put together different textures. Pair denim and silk, or leather and wool. Try things you would never normally wear, like a jumpsuit with a pair of heels, or short shorts with an amazing hat. It might look silly, or it could be your new fashion obsession. You'll never know until you give it a shot!

Pay attention to the things you seem to go for again and again. You will learn a lot about your personal tastes this way. I always go for an A-line skirt, anything pink, and my middle name might as well be magpie based on how fascinated I am by anything that sparkles!

See if you can figure out your patterns from the things you put in your style bible or on your vision board. The vision board in front of me right now has a watercolour painting by my friend Louise Androlia of a girl with a star on her forehead, a woman wearing a navy-blue turtleneck tucked into a 1950's style circle skirt, and a blonde wearing a white shirt, pink suit trousers, a pink coat, and black and white striped shoes. Yum! I spend so much time thinking about my style and tastes that I can tell in an instant how specific all of these things are to my own aesthetic. Each one of these images speaks volumes about my own style, the way I lean, and the things I go for.

When it comes to accessories, we all have things we obsess over more than others. For some of us it is belts, hats or handbags. For others it's shoes, make-up or legwear. I am pretty enamoured with all of the above, which makes life expensive and dangerous! Really though, I think that it's totally acceptable to go a bit nuts on accoutrements. The reason for this is simple: they dress up any outfit. You don't need as many clothes if you have a huge bureau full of things to spruce them up. A simple black dress can look completely different depending on the way you style it, which is why it's worth experimenting with these things.

I also maintain you should never throw any accessories out (unless they are broken or otherwise beyond repair). You never know when you'll need them. This is a lesson I've learned the hard way multiple times, and now, despite the fact that it makes moving house a really tooth-gritting adventure, I refuse to get rid of accessories. There is nothing more frustrating than thinking, 'Oh! I have a cuff which goes with this perfectly!', and then realising you threw it away in some misguided closet purge. Sad trombone!

Don't forget about inexpensive accessories, either. They are the best kind. You can buy such amazing, fun things for so little money, or you can make your own. I love to trawl through bead shops and make bracelets out of crystals. Like I said earlier, your wardrobe doesn't have to be constructed of million dollar items. Some of my favourite things cost me almost nothing or were free.

When it comes to shoes, however, going cheap is a mistake. You have to take care of your feet. Buy good shoes, and as much as you may love them, don't wear heels all the time. Break it up with boots or sneakers which are comfortable and well-made. Hobbling around isn't pretty, and long-term wear will eventually play havoc with your back. High heels are not worth permanent nerve damage!

* * *

MAKING IT EASIER TO GET DRESSED

It's hard to get dressed if you can't see what you own! You need to be able to survey your options with ease. This means, firstly, that you need to clear out your closet! Be ruthless! Sell or donate anything that you don't love, don't wear, or that doesn't fit.

♥ Make some space to display the jewellery, hats, and accessories you own. They should give you enough pleasure that you are happy to have them hanging on your wall! If they don't, it might be time to heave-ho. If you merchandise your clothing and accessories like you would in a store, getting dressed will become a much easier and much more pleasurable experience. We don't all have hundreds of square feet in which to drape every piece of clothing we own artfully over a mannequin, but if you can make a little room to give your clothing the space it needs, it will make an enormous difference.

♥ Consider planning your outfits at night. Pull them out of the closet and hang them on the door, so that when you wake up, they're the first thing you see. It sounds silly, but it can take a lot of pressure off your morning if you already know what you're going to wear. No clumping back and forth to the mirror with two different shoes on to check which one works best, no frantic hunting for a good bra, no panic about finding a pair of stockings without a big rip in the leg... Sounds like heaven, doesn't it?!

♥ Invest in a roll of Hollywood Tape. This is a fancy name for double-sided tape which comes in a pink box. (You can probably use double-sided tape in a pinch, though it may not be as sticky!) No exaggeration, though: it is a total lifesaver. I do not know how I existed without it. It's absolutely brilliant for keeping clothing in place, securing straps, and fixing hems which seem to fall just before you have to run out the door! I love it to keep a strapless dress in place, to get belts to stick in position, and even for keeping socks up! Buy some now. Use it all the time. It will rock your world just like it rocks mine.

♥ Discover the glory that is a good shoe insole. They are seriously incredible. They can make an agonising shoe wearable, keep a slingback on your heel, and make a too-big boot fit just right. They'll also pad your feet so that you don't get shocking reverberations all the way up into your skeleton. Like I said before, it's really important to take good care of your feet, so buy a bunch of insoles and throw them in all your shoes.

♥ Wear underwear which fits you and is flattering. I know this can be tricky, especially in a world where you can buy 5 pairs of underpants for $25, and even though they don't quite fit right, they were cheap, so you wear them anyway.

I am going to propose something wild. What I propose is this: let's not spend money on things which don't do the job. Take the time to buy underpants which fit you! This means they are comfortable; they don't cut in too tightly around the top of the leg or around the hip; they do not make you bulge like a sack of potatoes. Ill-fitting underwear can create lumps and bumps in even the most svelte creature. Good underwear makes you feel sexy and beautiful, which means it is totally worth taking the time and spending the money to get the stuff which fits!

You can't slip a beautiful dress on over too-tight panties and expect to look superb. It's just not going to work. This advice goes for bras tenfold. The right bra will lift you up, give you fab cleavage and not rise up in the back. It won't cut into you and make all your T-shirts look weird. It will make you look va-va-voom even if you have teeny tiny little booblets. For real. Good underwear is the way forward.

By the way, "magic underwear" really is. It comes in all kinds of different incarnations: some of them lift your bum and reduce your thighs, some tuck your tummy and some slim down your entire torso! Amazing. Every single celebrity wears these on the red carpet, so don't feel shy or weird about buying it! It exists for a reason!

♥ Invest in a full-length mirror and look in it EVERY TIME you get dressed. I don't think I need to explain this one!

HOMEWORK

❤ GO THROUGH YOUR CLOSET, AND BE RUTHLESS!

Time for a closet clean-out, my love. If it doesn't fit, is the wrong colour, is no longer your style, or you haven't worn it in the past year, it's gotta go! Sell it or donate it, and make space for something new and wonderful to come into your life.

❤ ASK YOURSELF: WHAT IS MY STYLE TELLING THE WORLD?

Again, be ruthless. If you can't objectively assess the messages your outfit is broadcasting, ask an honest friend. Do you like the implications of your aesthetic choices? If not, it's time to make a change!

❤ DISCOVER YOUR STYLE ICONS AND GET INSPIRED.

You might find your style icons anywhere: they could be from history, a character in a movie, or even someone from a book (Claudia Kishi, anyone?!). Print any photos that invigorate you and encourage you to take chances with your wardrobe. Ideally, put them all on a board near your closet for easy access to sartorial inspiration.

❤ TRY NEW THINGS!

If you've been a diehard goth for years, try wearing blue jeans. If you work at a country club, experiment with edging up your look. If you've never coloured your hair, dye it a revolutionary hue! You'll never know if you like it until you try… And luckily, few things are permanent!

❤ NEVER STOP CHANGING.

There are no rules when it comes to style, except one: never get stagnant. Variety keeps life fresh and juicy, so don't be afraid to flip the script on yourself… often!

Dress to make yourself happy, rather than attempting to chase perfection all the time. You will never get there, and there is no such thing as flawlessness.

#RSLBOOK

A GUIDE TO MANNERS FOR THE MODERN MINX

Etiquette, social graces and charming the pants off total strangers for the uninitiated!

FIRST IMPRESSIONS

Conventional wisdom exists for a reason: because it's the truth. That old saying about how you only have one chance to make a first impression is 100% correct. No matter how evolved we think we might be, we all judge a book by its cover, and a first impression goes far beyond what you're wearing or how much perfume you spritzed yourself with. First impressions are instinctual, natural, visceral. They keep us safe, and give us vital clues as to whether a person is trustworthy, or even someone we want to spend time with.

Think about all the people you've met in your life. Some of them just give you an unpleasant feeling straight off the bat, and that can be hard to shake. On the other hand, there are plenty of people who, as soon as you meet them, make you feel happy, comfortable, and at ease. Of course, you feel much more inclined towards those people in the future!

It's easy to talk about your impressions of other people, but how about their impressions of you? It can be difficult to take a step back and look at ourselves objectively, because, of course, we all want to believe that we are so dazzling that no one could possibly resist us!

However, it isn't always that cut-and-dried. You might be completely magnificent -- in fact, I'm sure you are! -- but other people don't know that. They might uncover it later on, but for now, you're just an unfamiliar face. They have no concept of who you are, where you've come from, what you're doing with your life, or whether you're interested in them at all. All they have to go on is your behaviour and the way that you treat strangers. So when you look at it that way, how do you think your first impressions would rank? Are you focussed, engaged, lit-up? Do you smile? Do you shake hands, hug, kiss? Do you make conversation or are you immediately searching the room for someone you know? All of these things add up to present a picture of who you are.

If you can keep that in mind -- that the people you meet have NO CLUE who you are, and that every time you meet a stranger, you are starting from scratch -- you will have a much better awareness of how you appear to them, which will empower you to be the very best you can be. Hopefully, it will help you make some new friends for life, or at least have them walk away thinking you're totally brill!

* * *

MEETING SOMEONE NEW

Some of us love to meet new people, while the rest of us are less amped on the concept. It can be kind of scary. What if they don't like you? What if you don't like them? What if there's nothing to talk about, or you make a huge, glaring social faux pas? Hey kitten, calm down. It's okay! I'm going to show you how to make the most of it!

If you feel awkward about meeting new people, don't worry, you're not alone. Even the most outgoing among us feel thrown by social outings from time to time, and it can be especially bad if you're in a foreign country and you're not quite sure how it's done. Should you nod and smile, shake hands, hug, kiss once, kiss twice, kiss three times? Should you actually touch cheeks or just air-kiss? That's just the first ten seconds! What a minefield!

As with most cultural traditions, the best thing to do is observe the people around you and take your cue from them. If there's no one around to take a hint from, you can either follow the other person's lead or just do whatever feels best. If you do it with enough confidence, the person you're meeting will just go along with it. (Having confidence is the secret of the universe.)

This might sound silly, but when it comes to shaking hands, a firm grip is very important. Not so firm that you Hulk out and grind the bones in their hand together -- no one likes that, it's rude, domineering, and unnecessary. But your handshake shouldn't be weak and limp like a dead fish, either. You want to aim for a happy medium, instead. People with a weak handshake tend to be thought of as being wishy-washy and non-committal, which definitely doesn't fall into the "positive first impression" category. You should also make eye contact while you do it, as this makes the other person feel that you are trustworthy and honest.

Why is the strength of your handshake so important? It's pretty trivial stuff, isn't it? Well, no. The American Psychological Association did a study which found that "those with a firm handshake were more extroverted and open to experience and less neurotic and shy than those with a less firm or limp handshake". Case closed: go practice your handshake!

As you shake hands, introduce yourself. "Hi, I'm Griselda" should do the trick, and be sure to look at them and smile when you say it! When they introduce themselves, you should repeat their name back to them. It will help cement their name in your head, and the sweetest sound to any person is their name, so don't be afraid to say it! The more you say it, the more they'll like you. This might sound crass and simple, but it works!

If you have trouble remembering names, use word association to lock it in. In your head, link them to someone famous who shares their moniker, or think of a word which rhymes with their name which seems to fit. Don't be afraid to ask people to repeat their names if you didn't quite catch it the first time. Much better to ask for clarification than to call someone the wrong name all night!

Usually you'll be introduced to a new person by somebody you already know, and if they stick around for a little bit, they can help facilitate the conversation. In fact, the best introductions happen when two strangers are given a little bit of information about one another from the get-go. If you're lucky enough to have this, take that tidbit and run with it! "Wow, so you work in aeronautics? That's so exciting -- how did you get started?" If you don't have anything to go on, however, you can start with the absolute basics. "It's great to meet you! How do you know so-and-so?"

Now that you know their name and have made a little physical contact, it's time to get down to the juicy stuff: making conversation, or as we say in New Zealand, "having a chin-wag"!

* * *

MAKING CONVERSATION

The real secret to being an awesome conversationalist is not to have a stack of hilarious stories squirrelled away. Nor is it to be the loudest, the funniest or the most open. The secret is learning to listen to other people. Shocking, I know. You might be thinking, 'How the hell does that help me become a better conversationalist?' The truth is that people only ever really want to talk about themselves. FACT.

It's not that shocking when you think about it, really. At the heart of things, most of us want to talk about the stuff that affects us! You are your own favourite subject, just as I am my own favourite subject. You want to talk about your hopes, wishes, and fears. You want to discuss your relationships, job, and health. You want to focus on your finances, drama, and problems. It has always been this way, and it will always continue to be, so if you, unlike most people, appear to enjoy listening to someone else, they're going to think you're pretty great.

Learn to become really interested in other people -- ironically, it is the only way to get them interested in you. (If you're not actually that interested in other people, you might just have to learn to fake it until you make it. After all, you don't want to be one of those crashing bores who only ever talks about themselves, right?)

Making conversation really is an art-form. There are tricks and verbal cues to hone in on, which tell you when to speak up and when to back off, when to ask another question and when to let the silence settle. While some people are born conversationalists, the rest of us require a little bit of practice, and that's really all it comes down to: practice! The great news is that you can practice on absolutely anyone and everyone, from your postman to your aunt, your co-workers to your yoga teacher.

All you need to do is learn how to ask questions. Don't get too personal, because most people don't want to divulge their deepest secrets to complete strangers, but make an effort to ask interesting questions! I think there's nothing worse than someone who immediately asks, "So, what do you do?" God, who cares. Ask me what I'm passionate about right now, or my latest vacation, or what I wanted to be when I grew up!

Generally, keep the conversation topics light but don't be afraid to delve into something juicy. Most manners experts would tell you to avoid talking about politics and religion, which is a good rule of thumb, but of course it depends on where you are and what you're doing. If you're looking to make friends at an anarchist rally or a church group, ignoring those subjects would just seem weird!

Avoid talking about the weather, unless there's something so shocking going on outside that it simply cannot be ignored (like a tsunami or an explosive volcano, and in that case, what are you doing at a party anyway?!). Ask questions which will get them to open up and explain things. If you want to get to know someone, you need to ask them open-ended questions, which means something they can't just respond "yes" or "no" to. This is the crux of interviewing people, too: ask them to elaborate on something, rather than just asking if such-and-such is true or false. You could ask them how they know the person throwing the party, compliment them on their outfit, or even just ask them how they're enjoying the event. Sometimes it just takes a statement with a bit of enthusiasm to kick-start a great conversation. "I'm so excited to be here, I have been waiting for this party for ages!" is so infectiously positive that most people will probably share a similar sentiment! Remember that enthusiasm and positivity are irresistible! Everyone wants to sit next to the person having a really good time.

If you have no idea where to begin, the best thing is to pick a topic and then find out their point of view. You can chip in with your opinion, of course, but most of the conversation should come from them. They'll come away thinking you're completely marvellous. You barely even need to contribute -- it's kind of like walking a dog. You just need to steer, and let them do the rest of the work.

I like to keep things upbeat and happy -- you'll never see me at a party grizzling about my day, my best friend, the food or some other triviality! Remember, people go to events like this to have a good time, and they don't want to get stuck next to someone who seems intent on grumbling about everything within a 20 metre radius! If you DID have a crappy day -- and hey, it happens -- try to put it aside. Don't bring it with you, because it does you no good, and -- harsh truth time -- no one really cares. Just be pleasant!

If you want to make a friend or even just a good first impression, it's totally your responsibility to make the conversation happen. Some people are shy and will need to be brought out of their shell a little bit. If you don't make the effort, they'll stay quiet and you're not going to create any kind of bond. Take the lead, be boisterous, and do your damnedest to be as outgoing as you can possibly manage. If you're not naturally this way (and don't worry, because a lot of us aren't), just pretend you are! Think of your super-extroverted friend, and do what you think they would do in this situation, or use one of your personal heroes as a role model. How would Beyoncé behave in this scenario? What about Prince or Bill Clinton? Visualise that, then act it out as best you can.

There is definitely an element of faking-it-until-you-make it here, which can make some people feel a little bit uneasy, but really, everyone feels like a bit of a phony when they're doing something for the first time. Before long, you'll be comfortable with making sparkling conversation with a whole range of people, and the little tricks or traits you have adopted from others will become more suited to who you are, and an easy, natural extension of your personality. It's only a matter of time, and again, practice.

Don't be afraid to approach strangers and start talking, especially when you're at a party or event. People go to those things for a reason, and it's usually because they want to see and be seen, meet new people and reconnect with old friends. Occasionally you will come across someone who isn't very charming, but you can't take that stuff personally -- maybe they had a bad day, or maybe they just have an unfortunate personality. That's really not your problem! Just move on to someone else.

Most people are totally thrilled to be approached by a stranger. They will feel excited, flattered to have captured your attention, and are really just delighted not to be standing in the corner by themselves anymore! My mother has always been great at approaching and including the shy people around the fringes of the room, and my father sometimes makes fun of her for it, because it's more his style to be standing in the middle of the room telling a story loudly and with great panache. But it just goes to show that we all have different socialising styles, and one is no better than another. Quiet people can congregate together, the story-tellers will gather somewhere else, and the people who just wanna dance will be over there, carving it up. It might take you a while to find the most natural, comfortable, enjoyable social tactics, but it's worth persevering, because as sure as the sky is blue, you will be invited to parties, and you can't hide in your bedroom forever!

If you're not a very social person, and generally prefer your own company to that of others, that's okay. You should still try and go out as much as you can. An insular life is all well and good, but you will learn much more, and your life will be much more exciting and expansive if you can let other people in a little bit. So when you accept an invitation, instead of regarding it with dread and freaking out about it, just decide to go for a short time. You don't have to go for four hours! Anna Wintour, editor of Vogue, goes to a party for just 15 minutes! It's enough time to walk in, say hello, do a lap, and split. Sometimes, that's all it takes... And you have to admire her efficiency!

It can also help to take a good friend, of course, and especially one who will introduce you to the most fascinating people! The more of this you do, the less harrowing it will feel, and before long, you might even be comfortable in a social environment. You just need to immerse yourself. You can do it!

* * *

100% CHARISMA ALL THE TIME

Charisma is an indefinable quality, but one definition that resonates with me is that when you're talking to a charismatic person, you will feel like the only person in the room. That's a rare and special feeling, and when it happens, you don't forget about it. That person will stand out in your head as someone exceptional, and someone whom you feel very positively towards.

A lot of people talk to others while simultaneously thinking of an exit strategy, or while scanning the room for their friend or someone famous. Don't be that girl! The person you're speaking to will feel unimportant, excluded, and disinterested, and they'll tune out from you very quickly. So if you're going to have a conversation, no matter how short, the very best thing you can do to amp up your personal charisma factor is to pay attention!

It's all very Eckhart Tolle when you think about it -- the key to being charismatic is simply being present. It sounds so basic, but so few people get it right. The first time my friend Dhrumil and I went out to dinner together, we discussed the importance of being present in a conversation. At one point, he said to me, "Think about it. Over the course of this dinner, you and I have probably made more eye contact than some married couples would in a week". That has always stuck with me. Eye contact is vital, and makes the other person feel important, valued, and engaged.

Making eye contact can be really hard at first, especially if as a child you were taught that it was rude to stare, or if you're not too hot in the radical self love department. This is not to mention that in many countries, avoiding eye contact with parents, elders, or people of a higher social status is taught as a form of respect. But if you're living in the Western world, getting comfortable making eye contact will be really valuable to you. All you can do is decide to work on it, and practice! Practice at the supermarket, the dry-cleaners, the deli. You might feel a bit strange about it at first, but you'll find that most people are extremely receptive. It's nice to think someone is actually paying attention to you, no matter how trivial the interaction.

Having said this, there are definitely times when you can take it too far. I used to have a boyfriend who had to train himself to look away from people, because otherwise they felt awkward, and told him he was "too intense". So there's a middle ground, of course!

Think about it, though: how awful does it feel to be engaged in a conversation with someone who acts as if they don't want to be there in the first place? In mild doses, it makes you feel uncomfortable, but when presented with an extreme example, you just want to throw a drink in their face while bellowing, "HOW RUDE!"

You want people to feel at ease, and to enjoy spending time with you. Conversation is a big part of this, but there are plenty of other subtleties which come under the heading of charisma which make all the difference.

Charisma is about magnetism, intensity, sex appeal, exuberance, great communication, sensitivity, empathy, being expressive, and bringing people together. Here are some ways to increase your personal charisma in a social setting.

♥ Don't be afraid to touch others. This doesn't mean you should offer them an impromptu shoulder massage, unless you're at, say, a rave. Instead, think about the ways that you can use touch to connect to other people. A lot of charismatic politicians will shake hands with their right, then use their left hand to touch the other person's elbow or shoulder. It's a way you can convey trust and a kind of intimacy. You don't need to do this, necessarily, but I mention it to encourage you to go a little beyond your comfort zone!

♥ Lean in towards the person you're speaking to. Leaning inward shows that you're interested, while leaning back or away from someone shows that you are passive and detached. On the flipside, if you lean in towards someone, they will tend to mirror your behaviour unconsciously, and invest themselves more in the conversation.

♥ Use metaphors liberally. A metaphor is when you say that one thing is something else, for example, the city is a snowglobe, her voice is music to my ears, or his heart exploded with fireworks. Studies have shown that the most charismatic leaders use metaphors much more often than the average speaker. Metaphors help draw a vivid picture in the listener's mind, and are a very compelling way of sharing information and inspiring others.

❤ Be passionate, which means don't talk about boring topics! People who are truly passionate are hard to resist: you can hear it in their voices and see it in their eyes. Talk about the things you love and value!

❤ Think about your tone. Sometimes, it's not the words you say, but how you say them. Record yourself speaking if you find it difficult to self-evaluate on the fly.

❤ Be aware of your body language. This subject is enormous, but a little bit of knowledge can take you a long way. For example, people with crossed arms are categorically not listening to you or taking what you say on board! If you want to know more about it, do some Googling, or pick up The Definitive Book Of Body Language by Barbara and Allan Pease, and be prepared to have your mind blown!

Charisma is really about showmanship and putting your best foot forward. It can seem almost like a performance if you don't do it with the best of intentions, so stay grounded, act with integrity, and be as personable as you can. Think of charisma as being yourself, just with the dial turned up several notches!

* * *

DALE CARNEGIE'S HOW TO WIN FRIENDS AND INFLUENCE PEOPLE

Dale Carnegie's book, How To Win Friends and Influence People, is one of the most popular books of all time. It was first published in 1936, was on the New York Times bestseller list for ten years, and sold over 16 million copies. Everyone has heard of it, but the craziest thing is how few people actually put the concepts of the book into practice!

The concepts are very simple, and I'll outline them here. For more detail, you should definitely buy yourself a copy. It's a quick read, but could be one of the most vital things you ever consume.

Fundamental Techniques in Handling People

1. Don't criticize, condemn or complain.

You might think you're right all the time, or that you know a better way of doing something, but ultimately, people don't really want to hear about it. Most people criticise themselves very infrequently, even when they're doing something horrible, because the human brain is capable of rationalising just about anything. Your critique will be totally unwelcome, and don't fool yourself into thinking otherwise! Criticism makes people feel defensive, resentful and hurt. Furthermore, they don't really want to hear about your problems, so curb the complaints. Harsh, but true!

2. Give honest and sincere appreciation.

Everyone wants to be told they're doing something well, to be encouraged and congratulated. When you enthusiastically compliment someone, it makes it almost impossible for them to dislike you -- unless, of course, they suspect you are being insincere! This is to be avoided at all costs!

3. Arouse in the other person an eager want.

If you know what people want or need, you'll be able to figure out a way to give that to them or otherwise help them out. If you don't know what gap needs filling or what a person's problem is, you'll be unable to provide them with a solution. People feel very positively towards those who have helped them in some way -- no matter how small!

Six Ways to Make People Like You

1. Become genuinely interested in other people.

As I said earlier, become interested in people other than yourself! Most people are only really concerned about themselves; if you encourage them to talk, they'll respond very positively to you!

2. Smile.

A good smile is heart-warming and makes people feel welcome and safe. You only have to look at how much the public critiqued Victoria Beckham and her past predilection towards pouting to see that someone who doesn't smile arouses suspicion and makes people wonder what's being hidden. So just smile! It makes the world a better place!

3. Remember that a man's name is to him the sweetest and most important sound in any language.

Don't you love it when people use your name? I know I do. It can take a while to feel natural using people's names, but just start small and work your way up. I like to address supermarket cashiers, waiters and anyone else wearing a tag by their name. It's a great place to begin.

4. Be a good listener. Encourage others to talk about themselves.

This is a total reiteration of my earlier point, which is that to be thought of as a great conversationalist, all you really need to do is guide the other person to talk about themselves. Ask pointed questions, listen to their concerns, and give them your undivided attention.

5. Talk in the terms of the other man's interest.

If you start a conversation by asking someone about themselves and the things that are important to them, you'll be hard-pressed to shut them up! Everyone loves to talk about their issues, so let them!

6. Make the other person feel important and do it sincerely.

If you recognise someone else's skill, they will feel good about themselves, and about you by extension. They'll also be likely to want to help you out, since it will give them another opportunity to prove how good they are. Respect people's authority and knowledge, and treat them as if they are important. Everyone is important in their own mind, and if you echo this back at them, they'll be so happy!

Twelve Ways to Win People to Your Way of Thinking

1. Avoid arguments.

Arguments are pointless: you will rarely change another person's opinion. In fact, after most arguments, both parties walk away feeling more sure of their own opinion than ever before. Even if you "win" an argument, the other person will probably resent you. No one ever really wins an argument!

2. Show respect for the other person's opinions.

Never tell someone they are wrong, as it is almost always equated with criticism in the mind of the listener. No one wants to be told they are wrong -- it hurts the ego and people's personal pride. Just listen to them.

3. If you're wrong, admit it quickly and emphatically.

It's easier to admit your guilt from the get-go than to let someone else start criticising you. Once they do this, most people will get on a self-righteous tangent which bolsters their own ego and will often derail to include a bunch of completely unrelated criticisms. If you say you're wrong, they won't have much to add.

4. Begin in a friendly way.

If you start a conversation with a compliment or something positive, it will disarm the other person and make it more difficult for them to rebuke you.

5. Start with questions the other person will answer yes to.

If you can get people to start saying yes, that momentum will drive them forward to get them to agree to other things too. Socrates was onto this one too, and said that the aim is to keep winning concessions until the other person is in a situation where they can't say no any more.

6. Let the other person do the talking.

...And don't interrupt them. Someone on a tangent isn't really listening to you anyway, so let them talk until they have nothing left to say, especially if they're angry. Let them talk the anger out, and don't jump in to defend yourself, because it will only escalate. Once they're finished, you can come back with a solution.

7. Let the other person feel the idea is his/hers.

Cater to their ego by letting them think that the solution came from them. Even if the solution isn't ideal for them, if they think it was their idea, they'll be much more receptive.

8. Try honestly to see things from the other person's point of view.

Most people never bother to do this. The more you can develop your own sense of empathy, the more likeable you will be. Really, all people want is to be understood by someone else.

9. Sympathize with the other person.

As above!

10. Appeal to noble motives.

People often have a variety of reasons for doing something. Some of these will be honourable, some less so. Appeal to the ones that they are likely to feel better about admitting to and they're more likely to go along with you. For example, people will be more willing to say that they support a charity because they believe in the cause than they will be to disclose that charitable donations give them a tax break!

11. Dramatise your ideas.

This is like in creative writing classes, where they say, "Show, don't tell". Draw a verbal picture, bring an example, or draw comparisons to help SHOW the other person what it is you mean. Make it exciting, vibrant, and visual. There's a great story about how SARK -- a self-help author known for her bright books and hand-lettering -- had to physically make her first book and take it to a publisher to show them what she envisioned. Give people a visual prompt.

12. Throw down a challenge.

Most people love to prove that they can do better than you think they can -- so appeal to their natural spirit for competition to get them to do what you're asking. Ask someone to enter into a friendly bet with you, or even run a contest among your friends.

Be a Leader: How to Change People Without Giving Offense or Arousing Resentment

1. Begin with praise and honest appreciation.

As above, if you begin on a positive note, it will put the other person at ease and relax them. It's easier to take criticism if you've been told you're good at something first -- it makes the blow feel less severe, and less like you're a hopeless wreck!

2. Call attention to other people's mistakes indirectly.

Rather than telling someone that something they've done is wrong, or saying their idea won't work, talk around the subject a little bit to make it easier for them to digest. You could say, for example, "I wonder how well this will work"... Give them the opportunity to present alternative ideas rather than dismissing what they have already done.

3. Talk about your own mistakes first.

This helps to humanise you and make you more relatable. Additionally, you're not claiming to be perfect, so the other person will feel less intimidated by admitting that they might have done something wrong.

4. Ask questions instead of directly giving orders.

If people feel they have a direct hand in making something happen, they will feel much more positive about it. It also gives people the opportunity to contribute their own ideas to the table, which might be brilliant! People crave autonomy, and the more they feel they have of it, the better their self-esteem, and consequently, the better their work ethic and effort.

5. Let the other person save face.

Just be nice. Don't reprimand someone in front of other people -- if it must be done, do it in private. Additionally, if you embarrass them, they will become resentful and much less willing to admit their mistakes.

6. Praise every improvement.

Be sincere and encouraging. If you're trying to alter someone's behaviour, it's far better to lavish praise on the positive than to rail against the negative. As you do this, their positive actions will continue to flourish, while their bad habits will eventually be replaced with better ones.

7. Give them a fine reputation to live up to.

If you tell someone how good you think they are, they'll be keen to prove you right.

8. Encourage them by making their faults seem easy to correct.

Don't be dramatic -- there's no sense in turning someone's flaw into the World's Worst Thing. Make it sound as if it's easy to change, and they'll feel empowered to do something about it.

9. Make the other person happy about doing what you suggest.

...By employing the above techniques!

If you've never heard of these tactics before, it can be a lot of information to take in. Write the highlights on an index card and put it somewhere you'll see it regularly, or in the place you do most of your work: next to your computer or phone is a great spot. Run your eyes over the card a few times a day, and make an effort to engage the techniques as much as possible. Before long, you'll be making friends and kicking ass all over the place!

THE GENERATION GAP, AKA THE CELLPHONE DILEMMA

While most people my age feel that it's normal to be glued to their cellphone at all times -- and sleeping with a phone under your pillow is the norm for many! -- it can be helpful to understand that not everyone feels this way.

When you're holding a cellphone aloft and you're out with your friends or family, it acts as a wall. People are so engaged by that little screen. Have you ever tried to get the attention of someone embroiled in a Very Important text message conversation? It's not possible; there's no way! People -- try as they might to prove otherwise -- are just not good multi-taskers. When your boyfriend's trying to give directions to his friend via text message, you could tell him that you want to start eating children, and he'd just grunt in approval!

Have you ever noticed that as soon as one person gets their phone out, everyone else starts to follow suit? That's because the conversation has started to shut down, and then everyone retreats into their own little world. It interrupts the flow of the discussion and once you've replied to your text or checked your email or whatever, you're not thinking about what's going on right in front of you any more. You're still processing your online life in your head.

This is not to say that you can't use your phone at dinner. Sometimes you'll get an important phone-call, and occasionally something will come up that genuinely needs to be attended to, but these moments are few and far between.

This all goes hand-in-hand with the charisma thing. It's about honouring the people you're spending time with by actually being present in the moment. If all your friends are compulsive phone freaks, maybe next time you go out to dinner, you could propose a no phone rule -- at least until you settle the bill. Some people will get twitchy, but you'll probably find that you'll all enjoy your evening much more if you give it a try!

*Having confidence is
the secret of the universe.*

#RSLBOOK

HOMEWORK

♥ PRACTICE BEING MORE CHARISMATIC.

Pick one thing to focus on -- maybe using touch to connect with others, or maintaining eye contact during a conversation -- and make it your mission for the week. Observe the way people respond to you, and if the reactions are positive, keep it up, and try one of the other suggestions!

♥ PUT DOWN YOUR PHONE.

I know how tempting it is to hold onto your phone at all times, just in case something exciting happens, but all this really achieves is keeping the present moment at arm's length. When you're engaged with your phone, you're only half-committing to whatever is going on around you. Give yourself the opportunity to connect with other people by leaving your phone at home sometimes!

♥WORK ON YOUR LISTENING SKILLS.

Remember that listening is not just waiting for your turn to speak! Even though your mind may be racing with thoughts, breathe slowly, and really listen to what the other person is saying. Make encouraging noises to demonstrate that you've heard what they said, and repeat it back to them afterwards!

♥AVOID ARGUMENTS.

They do no good. There is no "winning" an argument, so instead of getting fired up, choose to simply side-step them, instead.

♥ FOCUS ON MAKING WHOEVER YOU'RE TALKING TO FEEL GOOD.

This is a beautiful one to close with, and ties back to the rest of Radical Self Love: A Guide To Loving Yourself And Living Your Dream so nicely. It's such a simple truth: if you can focus on making yourself and other people feel really good, you can't lose.

CONCLUSION

Sometimes I'm asked why radical self love is important. After all, the proliferation of selfies from this generation would surely indicate that everyone thinks pretty highly of themselves! My answer is that until women stop apologising for existing, until eating disorders are a thing of the past, and until we stop giving our power away, we are going to need radical self love... in enormous doses.

We don't learn how to love ourselves from any conventional source. It's not a subject in school. As we grow up and stumble out into the world, we look around at our friends and realise that it's "normal" to hate what you see in the mirror, to feel directionless, to seek solace in drugs, alcohol, and dysfunctional relationships.

It makes me furious that this is something we're supposed to figure out on our own. Unless you're prepared to devote yourself to the subject, how do you even start? There is no roadmap, which can make self-love seem like a Sisyphean task. Hopefully, Radical Self Love: A Guide To Loving Yourself And Living Your Dream has remedied that, by shining a little light so that you know where to begin.

A common misconception is that radical self love is self-serving or narcissistic. It's not. Having gratitude for your body, being able to accept a compliment, and making an effort to seek out things that nourish your soul rather than your ego are all good things. They're positive things. But the goal is not to become a one-babe appreciation party. Ultimately, the goal of radical self love is to move it outside of yourself and into the world. One of the most important things we can do, once we've discovered how to love ourselves, is to show others what we've learned. I believe in sharing information, and leading by example.

Think: if I was being a #radicalselflovewarrior today, how would I behave? How would I act, and what would I do? Make an effort to be a positive role model for others. Behave with integrity, and act out of love. Be honest, be kind, be thoughtful.

Don't keep radical self love to yourself. Use it to help others. Volunteer at a charity or mentor someone else. In fact, one of the best ways to make ourselves happy is to do something for someone else!

I've been learning, researching, and doing radical self love experiments for over eight years now. It's not always easy. There are a lot of challenges that come up when you do this kind of work. But I keep going, because I know it's not about me. It's about the people who hear the message and take it to heart.

We learn so much of what it means to be a woman from our mothers, and my greatest hope for the future is that the next generation of mothers will walk the radical self love walk so powerfully that their children won't be able to help learning by example. My dream is that these women will be well-equipped to teach their children about self-love, self-respect, and creating a life of beauty. Maybe they'll make gratitude lists together over breakfast; maybe they'll tap before bedtime; maybe it'll be as simple as refusing to body-shame yourself or others. My greatest wish is that this next generation will grow up with more tools to help them cope with their emotions; to squish their fears and go on to do amazing things.

Life is what you make it. I am convinced that there is no one-size-fits-all meaning to life: the meaning is whatever you bring to it.

Don't make the popular mistake of thinking that your fate is predestined; that you are subject to the whims of a cruel universe. Nothing could be further from the truth! In fact, the opposite is true. The universe is conspiring to shower us with blessings, as Rob Brezsny says. I want you to realise that nothing in life is set in stone, and this is a wonderful thing. It's a gift. Life is limber and flexible, and we can stretch it and bend it at will.

You always have the choice. You can fill your day with magic or let traffic sour your mood; enjoy a moment of peace or be annoyed at your friend's tardiness; take a risk or play it safe. Your fate is in your own hands, and it will be determined by the decisions you make.

I have total faith in you. So what if your friends don't get you, your family is pessimistic, and even your dog sometimes looks at you, like, 'Damn, what is UP with you?!' None of that matters. I have your back! All of the most fantastic people from history have faced opposition. In fact, you could say that if no one has tried to tear down your idea, it's not big enough. You don't need anyone's permission or acceptance to go out there and do you. All you have to do is begin.

The most beautiful thing in the world is someone living to their fullest potential.

Please share your findings, discoveries, and general bad-assery on the #rslbook hashtag. I'm so excited to connect with you, learn about your life, and bear witness as you travel along the path of radical self love!

You're a shining star. I love you, and I'm proud of you.

Kisses,

Gala

The most beautiful thing in the world is someone living to their fullest potential.

#RSLBOOK

IF YOU ENJOYED THIS BOOK AND WANT MORE:

♥ Visit my blog: galadarling.com

♥ Follow me on Twitter and Instagram: @galadarling

♥ Join my Facebook community: facebook.com/xogaladarling

♥ Check out these hashtags on Instagram: #rslbook #galadarling #radicalselfielove #radicalselflovecoven

Radical Self Love Bootcamp is my six-week course designed to shake, rattle and roll your perceptions about yourself. Join hundreds of other women and change your life for good! galadarling.com/radical-self-love-bootcamp

Gala Darling is available for select readings and lectures. To inquire about a possible appearance, please contact love@galadarling.com.

Printed in Great Britain
by Amazon.co.uk, Ltd.,
Marston Gate.